YOU MIGHT BE AN ASSHOLE...

Praise for You Might Be an Asshole but It Might Not Be
Your Fault

"Dr. Katie Ervin's leadership training has made a tremendous impact on our city's emerging leaders over the past two years. I don't know if we've had any Mikes in our classes, but I do know that the journey described in this book is one that all of us need to go on. Katie's approach is so spot on for today's current and future leaders, and I believe the lessons in this book can positively impact your managers' competence and your employees' experiences."

--Jim Bowers
Human Resources Director, City of Lenexa

"Dr. Katie takes us on a journey where learning is around every corner. Whether you are a seasoned leader who could use some leadership skill sharpening or a new leader looking for what makes you effective, this is a must-read and one you'll enjoy every step of the way."

--David Brzozowski
Director of Training w/TalentSmartEQ

"It's no secret that the landscape of leadership and culture is changing. What is wonderful about this book is it is a cornucopia of practical tools and applications. Dr. Katie has done a fantastic job of relaying her litany of expertise in the culture and leadership arena. You can take this book and immediately begin shifting the atmosphere in your places in influence."

--Brad Hill
Executive Director, HeartConnexion Seminars

"*You Might Be an Asshole* is a straight-forward fable that reinforces the misconception that the 20% of intolerable employees who deliver 80% of revenue and productivity are never worth the human capital cost in the form of employee turnover, reputation cost - which comes from arrogantly overpromising and with no consideration of deliverability and turning a blind eye to bad behavior. It makes leaders reflect on their role in creating assholes in the workplace.

In addition to the unintentional consequence of prioritizing revenue over the whole team approach, throughout *You Might Be an Asshole* you'll find familiar anecdotes of the different ways leaders contribute to stifling the growth of their team and themselves by not consistently seeking out feedback and opportunities for improvement. Leadership is a journey. I believe it is safe to say many of us look back at our leadership journey and cringe at who we were at times. That is OK as long as we continue to grow through the challenges we go through."

--Cass Butler Dunlap, PhD
Coaching Operations Leader, Positive Intelligence

"If you have worked even a day in your life, you will resonate with the stories Dr. Katie shares in her book to demonstrate the critical importance of preparing leaders to lead. Self-awareness is the key to effective change, and if you might be being an asshole, don't you want to know? With authenticity and kindness, Dr. Katie helps you identify your potential blindspots and models what effective and aligned leadership in the workplace looks like.

--Maki Moussavi
Author of *The High Achiever's Guide*
Mindset and Executive Coach

"If I had to sum up this book in two words, I would say creative and impactful. The structure of the book is unique and highly engaging. I love how we follow Mike's journey from being an asshole to learning how to truly be a leader. Having that case study really drives home the educational content provided in each chapter. Not to forget the reflection questions that give individuals the chance to self-reflect on where they are in their journey to being an impactful leader. I highly recommend this book to anyone who wants to improve their leadership skills."

--Sertrice Grice
Co-Author of Inclusalytics.
Chief Consulting Office and Co-Owner of Mattingly
Solutions

"This riveting story of Mike, a person we have all met, will capture you from word one. It's a little bit Patrick Lencioni style, with a good dose of doing the right thing, and has all the right ingredients to be a leadership book "must-have" for any leader trying to get better. What's even better, each chapter contains leadership learnings and discussion questions to immediately apply. I blew through this book and am still thinking about it."

--Lynn Parman
Chief Operating Officer, National Association of Intercollegiate Athletics
You Might Be an Asshole but it Might Not Be Your Fault

You Might Be an Asshole...

But It Might Not Be Your Fault!

The guide to good leadership that will work for anyone.

DR. KATIE ERVIN

Catalyst Development

You Might Be an Asshole but it Might Not Be Your Fault
Copyright © 2023 by Dr. Katie Ervin

Catalyst Development
Dr. Katie Ervin
katie@cdleaders.com

You Might Be an Asshole but it Might Not Be Your Fault––1st ed.

ISBN: 979-8-218-17407-1

Cover Design by Emma Blankenship

Dedication

This book is such a labor of love and history. I am so excited to share it with you all. It is not possible with many people!

To my husband, Rob, thank you for being on this wild ride with me. I love that you are always up for an adventure and willing to "hear me out" when I have a crazy idea. I love you!

To my amazing kids, Abby and Drew, you all mean so much to me. Thank you for your patience with me on my journey of growth. You inspire me each day to do more and be better.

To my right and left arms, Emma and Jenna, I could not do what I do without you. Thank you for trusting me to take a left turn and believing in my dream. Without you filling my gaps, Catalyst would not be where it is today. I am truly grateful for you both!

To those who will not be named but inspired the stories in the book, my hope for all of us is that we all learn from our mistakes and missteps. We do not need to be perfect; we just need to learn from the opportunities that are put in front of us.

Introduction

Often in organizations, we have great workers who we reward with a promotion. Unfortunately, too often with the promotion, we don't provide them with leadership training, and then we are disappointed if they are not successful in supervising people or moving from a front-facing role to a more strategic role. It is through the lack of training and support that someone can be mistaken as an asshole. Most of the time asshole behavior is small. It is not always as blatant as it is in this book. Spotting bad behavior takes kind conversations, self-awareness, and internal reflection.

Along with my work experience, my doctoral research area is workplace motivation and employee satisfaction. Specifically, I wanted to know how we are motivated to complete work. In employee satisfaction, I studied happiness, engagement, effectiveness, and loyalty. When we find ways to support our people, they are satisfied and more motivated to work. We spend way too much time at work to not be fulfilled by it.

My research led me to discover the Self-Determination Theory (SDT) of motivation by Deci and Ryan (1985). I love this theory because it does not look at motivation as a whole but looks at it as a continuum. Depending on the environment and/or tasks we can be more or less intrinsically motivated to complete the task. It is not all or nothing.

The beauty of doctoral research is you look at *much* of the research in your area. Through my research, I was shocked to see very limited use of SDT in the workplace. That led me to create the Catalyst Workplace Model. The model focuses on people's basic needs in the workplace. Those needs are to feel like they belong and can show up as their true self——and that they have the tools and training to do their job successfully. Finally, they have the autonomy to complete their job. This model can be visualized as interlocking gears. For people to be happier, more loyal, and work at a higher level of productivity, they must have all three.

In order to create an opportunity where people are set up for success, leaders are key! Strong leaders can create the environment for all of this to happen. I tease, this is not hard, but it can be challenging. It takes very intentional work. Everyone is not a born leader. Plus, we can still work to build our leadership skills even if you are.

Leadership skills are incredibly important at all different levels——no matter which stage or level we are in our career. The topics stay the same but the conversations around them are different. We can all focus on who we are as a leader, how we communicate, create an environment of belonging, build strong teams, be more efficient, and be resilient.

I learned early in my HR career that when we promoted people who performed well in their roles and did not train them, more often than not they were not successful when they began leading people. Leading people seems so common sense but the problem with common sense is it is only common if we teach it. This is when I created the outline which is now my Catalyst L.E.A.D.E.R.s. program and which is weaved throughout this book.

The Catalyst L.E.A.D.E.R.s. program is an intentional leadership skill program that no matter where someone is on their career journey, they can focus on these career and power skills. There are six umbrellas with six career and power skills tucked in them. These skills are laid out at the back of the book.

In the L.E.A.D.E.R.s. program the little "s" is "so what"! What should you do with what you learn? At the end of each chapter, you will find "Be the Catalyst" nuggets. These are lessons learned or tools for you to use. Some of these are bigger than others. I hope that at the end of each chapter, you take a moment to pause and reflect on your path to leadership.

A catalyst is an agent that produces change or action. We can all step up to build a better workplace. For me, it is all about the people! This is a chance for you to decide what leadership is about for you. My wish for you is to be a self-aware leader that positively impacts those you come in contact with.

As you read *You Might Be an Asshole but It Might Not Be Your Fault*, there will be times when you think, there is no way that happened, or someone said that. Unfortunately, the situations and shocking statements are 100% true. Details of exactly what happened have been changed to protect the guilty. As you read through the book, please know that I pride myself on being honestly kind. In all these situations that impacted me, I had a direct, kind, and caring conversation with the person involved. Some cared, and some did not.

Throughout the upcoming chapters, we follow Mike through his leadership development journey. This story could be many of us as we work our way through our path to leadership. Whether we're just starting in our careers or seasoned leaders, it is important for us to continue to learn and grow. The organization Mike joins is an extremely healthy organization. I acknowledge this is not all organizations. It takes intentional work to build a safe and healthy workplace. I also acknowledge that in this story, Mike is in sales. Bad leadership is not isolated to one type of work or person. If we don't grow as leaders, we can all unintentionally be assholes.

If you are like me, I often pick up a book looking for tips to use in business or help a friend. I truly hope you will take the time to reflect on who you are as a leader by journaling the reflective questions at the end of each chapter. Whether we want to admit it or not, we all have times in life that we are not proud of. These are the times when we can either blame someone else, make excuses for our behaviors, or grow from them. It is up to you how you handle them.I

Chapter 1

How Did I Get Here?

Mike is sitting in a dark, full, loud local pub. It is the kind of place where you can enjoy a great burger with your work team during the week and cheer on your favorite sports team on the weekend. But this night is special.

It is time for the annual corporate celebration, and Mike sits on a barstool looking over the room. This is not what it normally looks like. Usually, this celebration is in a fancy hotel banquet room with an expensive plated dinner, but this year is different. It is Mike's twenty-fifth work anniversary celebration; but more importantly, it's his last, as he's retiring in two weeks. He looks out over the room of colleagues, friends, mentors, peers, and his family. He laughs as he thinks about the messy journey that he took to get himself here.

When he was younger, he was a hard, driven, eager salesperson, and a self-proclaimed bachelor. He didn't need anyone slowing him down on his path to becoming a millionaire. He shakes his head and grins now as he takes a moment to reflect on the important pivot that he took early in his career. The situation that changed his career path was somewhat out of his control, but it was important because it was when he realized that he was not the leader or person he wanted to be.

Early on, he had a reputation for stepping on people, burning relationships, and getting the sale at any cost. He didn't have an understanding of what holistic success looked like. He thought success was just about money and titles. He recalls one time when he was a vice president, and he demanded his own parking spot. *What an asshole!* Through a long journey, he learned that success has everything to do with relationships, strong teams, and humility.

As Mike sits quietly, smiling and reminiscing, his dear friend Allison, the company CEO, sits next to him. She elbows him in the side and tries not to look hopeful.

"You're quiet, what's going on? Have you decided not to retire?" Allison asks.

"No, I am just taking this all in," Mike responds. "Can you believe it?"

"You've come a long way and done so many great things," Allison says. "When we met, I could never imagine this is where we would be!"

"I have been reflecting on my time with the organization and our chance meeting that changed my whole path to leadership." Mike pauses and shakes his head. "I had so many failures early in my career. Thank goodness you let me know I was being an asshole!" He chuckles.

Allison smiles knowingly. "It was not easy. You were stubborn, but you finally got it."

"Thank goodness. Lord knows what this room would look like if I didn't change!" he says. "Actually, I do know. I wouldn't be here."

Allison smiles because she had a similar path, and if someone didn't convey the importance of being a strong leader, she would not be where she is today either.

"I'm proud of you, Mike," she shares. "You've been by my side for quite some time growing this leadership team and this company. We wouldn't be here without you."

There's an outburst of laughter at a table nearby, and both Mike and Allison watch fondly as one employee tells an animated story to the rest of the group. Their organization is thriving, not just in the city but in the whole region. They are having financial success, but most importantly, they are building strong leaders with low turnover. The team helped build the company to where it is today. Employees believe in the mission and enjoy the work they're doing.

"Soak it all in, Mike," Allison reminds him. "The success you've achieved is because of your hard work, as well as the hard work of everybody in the room."

Mike's wife Grace walked over to check in on him. She could not believe how many people were in the room. Their three kids and seven grandkids had also flown in for this exciting night.

"What are you two talking about in the corner?"

"I was trying to talk him out of retiring. How are we going to work without him?" Allison replies.

Mike smiles, knowing exactly what Grace's response would be.

"Oh, no! We have a cruise booked at the end of the month, and we might not ever come back."

They all laughed and then joined a group at a nearby table. The owner of the bar came over to thank Mike and the group. "We are so happy to have you all here tonight," the owner says. "You all keep me in business with your pizza parties, happy hours, and group outings."

This was one of their favorite places. It held so many memories.

Yet, as important as it is to celebrate Mike's success, we must understand where he started and how he got here, so let's start from the beginning.

Be the Catalyst

Everyone is on their own career journey! Who we are at 18, 27, 45, or 63 is a culmination of our experiences. When we choose to have a growth mindset, it allows us to learn from our mistakes and grow from our challenges. We need to reflect on our past and not be bogged down by our missteps. We cannot live in what could have or should have happened!

Career journeys are also winding roads. We do not have straight paths as we move through our careers. It is ok to have missteps and to grow from them.

Reflection

- How would you describe your career journey? Has it been a clean straight line? Or does it resemble a winding river through a dense forest?
- What have been your greatest triumphs and challenges?
- At the end of your career, what do you want your impact to be?

Chapter 2

The Early Years

Mike grew up in the suburbs of a fairly big Midwest town. He was the older brother to two sisters. Both of his parents were highly successful businesspeople who attended college and held MBAs. His parents had very high expectations for the whole family. His dad would often say, "You must be the best, and we won't settle for anything else!"

Mike played soccer since he could walk. When he was seven, he joined a travel club that practiced year-round and traveled to tournaments at least once a month. He never forgot how one day his dad got thrown out of one of his soccer games. Mike was not playing well, and his dad kept yelling at him, "Play harder, push more, and shoot the ball!"

His dad even screamed at the referees about fouls and other kids' "dirty" play. Mike was not sure how to feel about this. He was a bit embarrassed, but also this was all he knew. His father's behavior had become predictable, and it applied a lot of performance pressure on Mike. At half-time, the coach approached the sideline and asked Mike's dad to tone it down. The referees had warned that the team would be disqualified if he did not stop. Five minutes into the second half, his dad yelled at Mike, "You're embarrassing yourself and your family!" The head referee stopped the game and said, "You're out of here, Dad. You need to go relax and realize these kids are seven years old." His dad was furious and took Mike off the field. As

Mike and his dad walked away, Mike heard a parent say, "What an asshole!"

Mike continued to work hard at soccer to please his father. As he grew older, he found that he wasn't sure if he was having fun, but he did know it made his dad happy. He played in club teams, practiced year-round, and frequently missed social events because of soccer. His hard work paid off. He made the varsity soccer team his freshman year of high school and was even a starter for a very demanding coach. Everyone else complained that the coach was cutthroat, but Mike never saw it. He knew if he worked hard, the coach would like him and would play him more.

In his sophomore year, Mike was running down the field and passed to an open teammate, to which his dad yelled, "Stop passing the ball and shoot on the goal!" Mike thought to himself *"Huh, I guess this is what high school soccer is."* Throughout the rest of his high school games, his dad continued to yell "Shoot the ball," so Mike thought it was okay to not pass the ball to any of his teammates. He broke the school's record for the most goals scored in his senior season.

The team went to the state finals that year, and toward the end of the game, the score was tied. In the last thirty seconds, Mike had the decision to make: pass the ball to an open teammate who had a wide-open goal or take the shot. He knew what he was capable of and decided this was his time.

He said to himself, *"I'm going to take that shot."* He hit it as hard as he could, and the goalie made a miraculous save. Mike's team did not win the state championship. After the game, Mike was so upset with his teammates. *"Why were they not there to back him up on his shot on goal?"*

In the locker room, his teammates were furious at him. They accused him of being selfish. "You are not a team player, man. You blew this for us." Mike heard someone mumble something about him needing to learn to be humble.

"Who has the most goals on this team?" Mike shouted. "Remember, I hold the record." By now he was red in the face. "We wouldn't have even been in this game if it weren't for me!"

"You don't have to be an asshole!" another teammate said as Mike stormed out of the locker room.

When it came time to go to college, Mike chose a prestigious business school in the Midwest. Mike jumped right into his classes. He got involved in a fraternity and tried out for the soccer team but didn't make it. He was so upset he asked to speak to the coach.

"Coach, I think there was a mistake. I am way better than most of the guys on the team."

"Well, Mike, I am afraid to tell you, that is the problem," Coach explains. "That is why we can't have you on the team."

"That is ridiculous. I led my team to state my senior year and broke the school record of goals scored," Mike replies.

"Yes, but during tryouts, you rarely, if ever, passed the ball. Even when your teammates had an open goal, you choose the more difficult shot. You missed the goal several times because of that," Coach says.

"You can't listen to rumors. Give me a chance. I deserve it. I have been working hard for this!" Mike pleads.

"Mike, I am sorry. We don't have a spot this year. Keep working and try out next year. Or you can do intramurals and just have fun playing," Coach adds.

Mike was angry because he didn't think the coach understood who he was and didn't see all his hard work. Instead of reflecting on the coach's comment about teamwork and having fun, Mike dove into his fraternity and made many friends. Mike led his fraternity's intramural soccer team and also coached one of the sorority's intramural teams. Often people would say to him "Man, this is supposed to be fun. Take it easy." This frustrated him. *Why play if you're not going to play hard?*

In his senior year, he became president of the fraternity, and his hard-edged ways were encouraged by the outgoing president, who advised Mike that he needed to stay on top of everybody.

"You can't expect them to do hard work," the outgoing president shared. "You've got to tell them what to do. You've got to assign tasks and hold them to it, even if you have to push them."

Mike stepped into the role with pride and quickly started issuing jobs and responsibilities, including implementing checklists. He let everyone know what they needed to do. When people didn't do what he asked of them, he would put them in "timeout" and not include them in activities. Often his lackluster fraternity brothers would be assigned the worst jobs in the house.

By the end of his senior year in college, he found that many of the fraternity members were not showing up at events and meetings. In the spring, he yelled at them during a chapter meeting, letting them know that they would not win the campus awards and their national fraternity awards if they didn't participate and get their jobs done. "If you don't start showing up, you will be fined and put on probation," he chided. Tired of his bullying ways, many people dropped out or ghosted the fraternity. For the first time in seven years, they did not win any of the awards.

However, other things were in play for Mike's future. In the fall of Mike's senior year, his dad visited with several family friends and golfing buddies. Three of the guys in the group were vice presidents at the same very large company in their hometown.

"Mike, how is school?" VP #1 asks. "What are your plans?"

"It's good! I am ready to be done and get to work making some money. People here just don't get it," Mike explains.

"I hear you. I hated college, but it introduced me to these two guys," VP #2 points at the other two VPs. "I am not sure I would have gotten the job without them."

Mike adds rather brashly, "I hope you guys have a spot for me!"

VP #3 jumps in quickly. "We already discussed it with your dad, and you will be a good addition to our organization. Just let us know when you're ready, and we'll get you started."

Mike graduated in the spring toward the top of his class, and before he graduated had a very prestigious sales job with his dad's friends' company in his hometown.

Be the Catalyst

No matter where we are in our careers or our personal lives, we are exposed to behaviors that create an imprint on who we are and how we move forward in our lives. This starts early in life. When we see toxic behaviors or our unhealthy behaviors are not corrected, we might assume that it is acceptable. Too often, bad behavior appears to be rewarded because someone does not want to confront the behavior for one reason or another.

It can be scary to speak up when we see bad behavior. Accountability is key for us and others. Building relationships matter.

Reflection

- How are you modeling the behaviors of those around you?
- Are these behaviors having a negative or positive effect on those around you?
- What changes in your behavior might you need to explore?

Chapter 3

The New Job

After graduation, Mike jumped right into his new job. On the first day of work, he strutted into the office of Joe, the vice president of sales. Joe had been at the company for fifteen years and had known Mike since he was five. Joe was his dad's golfing buddy and was the VP who had promised Mike the job when he visited him at the college football game. Mike was excited to work for Joe and looked at him as a mentor.

As Mike glanced around the office, he noticed that Joe's office was full of stuff! Awards on the wall from being the top salesperson, gifts from clients on his desk, and pictures of him with influential people on his bookshelves. Joe was very well dressed and *always* in fancy suits. Mike knew this about Joe, so before his first day at work, he went shopping to upgrade his clothes. He bought an expensive suit and shoes that he really could not afford. *I will make the money back quickly,* he thought! He was not sure he could keep up with Joe's style, but he was willing to try.

Joe stood up immediately when he saw Mike and gave him a big hug. "It is so great to see you! I am excited for your first day!"

"How do I look?" Mike asks. "I had to go buy a new suit to keep up with you!"

Joe laughs, "You have a long way to go, kid, but I will get you there! The first thing to learn in sales is to work hard and play hard! Win at all costs!"

"I will follow you around and take notes," Mike adds.

Joe handed Mike a notebook. "We are going to hit the ground running after lunch, so be ready."

With that, Mike's orientation was over. All he knew was that he was expected to go out, make sales, and bring them back. Mike was a little uneasy. *How will I know what to do? I don't even know anything about the products I am expected to sell.* Mike trusted Joe which gave him a little bit of confidence. By the end of his first day, they had attended three different client meetings. It was a very busy day.

However, Mike was worried as he got back to his desk and gathered his things to leave. He felt a little panic. *Can I do this job? I don't think I know what I'm doing!* As he was deep in these thoughts, Joe walked past his desk.

"Are you coming back tomorrow?" Joe jokes.

Mike hesitated and then says, "I'm a little nervous. Am I going to be able to do this? There is a lot to learn, and I am not sure how I am going to understand all the products that we offer. How did you learn it?"

"Look, there is a lot to our products, and it is not our problem. Find out what the client's needs are and then let them know we will find a way to make it happen for them. Just get the sale," Joe advises.

Mike took Joe's advice to heart and began making sales. As time went by, Mike made lots of good friends outside the company and was known as the party guy. However, he was not making friends within the company. He could not make a connection with the team, and he wasn't sure why. From the outside looking in, however, it was easy to see why. A joke among other people on the team was that Mike would sell the dream, and everyone else would have to deliver the nightmare.

He didn't understand what his colleagues did, and at the end of the day, he felt it didn't matter. As long as he made the sale, he looked good. *That's what Joe said, right? Why should he think any differently?*

The tension between Mike and the team became more serious the longer Mike was with the company. Mike would yell at the product team if they said they could not fill an order. He often threatened that if they could not do their job, they should be replaced. No one was sure if Mike had this kind of power, but they also were not sure if they wanted to find out. He would tell them that he was going to go to the president to say that they weren't capable of doing their job. Many people knew his behavior was toxic, but because he was making so much money for the company in his sales, they were not sure that HR or the president would ever fire him.

During a product team meeting, there was a discussion among the group about the issues they were experiencing. The team vented their frustrations. "Mike can be such an asshole!" The team leader told them that he had been having discussions with their VP of products as well as with Joe, the VP of sales. The team leader told his employees desperately, "I am trying to get Mike under control, but we have to walk a fine line. He brings us so much business, and we don't want to run the risk of him leaving."

Over the next several months, the product staff slowly began finding other jobs and left the company. It was becoming obvious to Human Resources that there was some kind of issue in the product team. *Why were so many people leaving?* The company did not do an official exit survey, and no one leaving spoke up about their concerns. Within their ranks, however, members of the product team spoke openly to each other. Those who left felt that Mike's behavior was so well-known and tolerated it would do no good for them to speak up. When they submitted their resignations, they would simply remark that they had a better opportunity. Sometimes, it was about more money, and the other excuse often noted was that they were leaving for personal reasons.

Even with the exodus of many people on the production team, at one point, Mike quipped that he could say or do anything he wanted because he was a top sales guy. "They'll never fire me," he said. "They have too much to lose!" His peers who heard this were shocked and disappointed. Unfortunately, this was all too true! At one point, someone did go to Becky, the HR director, and complained about Mike's behavior. Becky was so upset hearing that Mike was bragging about getting away with horrible behavior that she immediately went to talk to Joe.

Becky knocked on Joe's door, which was slightly closed. She could see he was working at his desk.

"Hey, Joe. Do you have a minute to discuss something important?" Becky asks.

"I am pretty busy, but I can spare a little time for you." Joe looked up from his computer.

Hoping she could convey the seriousness of the matter, Becky walked in and clicked the door closed behind her. She sat down across from Joe and sighed. "We've been getting complaints about Mike and his boastful, often ridiculing behavior toward some of our staff," says Becky. "This could cause a big problem for the company if it continues."

Joe laughs, "Look, we all know Mike has an ego, but he is good at his job. People just need to figure out how to work with him!"

"It would be wise to bring this matter to his attention," adds Becky as she rose from the chair to leave, a deep look of concern etched on her face.

When Becky left the office, she immediately sought out Sheila, the president. Becky was hesitant because she knew that Sheila valued the money Mike brought into the company, but she also knew she had to say something. This had to be dealt with. She told Sheila about the problems that they were having with Mike and Joe.

"We cannot afford to lose Mike or Joe," Sheila remarks. "They're paying our company's bills. Their sales are equal to the rest of the sales team's results. If we let them go, we would not be able to maintain our current level of revenue."

"But what if we lose other key employees because of them?" Becky asks pointedly. "That would have an impact on sales, too!"

Sheila shrugs. "Perhaps, but my guess is that we'd risk losing clients who would eagerly follow Mike or Joe to another company."

Becky shook her head in dismay.

"You and your team will just have to figure out how to calm the waters around Joe and Mike," Sheila advises.

Over the next couple of years, Mike and Joe's behaviors did not change. The company experienced higher turnover in every area except for sales. The company also started losing clients because they weren't able to get the product that was promised to them or the service that they expected. The losses were mounting. Replacing the employees alone topped in the millions of dollars. It cost more and more to replace people because the company had a reputation for churning and burning employees. The loss of sales only compounded the problem.

With the company in decline, the president became upset with everybody. At one meeting, Sheila chastised her executive team as well as the senior leadership. "Mike and Joe are out selling and bringing in new business, and the rest of the organization is sabotaging their hard work. What do you plan to do about it?"

About a year later, the company was in serious financial trouble because it could not retain any good employees. In fact, they couldn't even keep the ones who stayed. Layoffs began. Sheila was insistent that Joe and Mike were to remain in the company because they were the ones bringing in all the business. The company held on for another seventeen months before it eventually closed. Joe and Mike went to a competitor, taking all their clients with them.

Be the Catalyst

I am often frustrated by organizations that say "They leave for more money" when someone quits. Sometimes that is true but often it is about culture and bad leadership. I am a firm believer that if a recruiter calls you and you are happy, they will never get to the money discussion. I have never talked to a recruiter who led with "We are going to pay you $10,000 more." When a recruiter calls, they usually ask "Are you interested in an opportunity?" If you are happy and content with your job, you will rarely listen to opportunities. When people are not happy in their situation is when they will tell the recruiting that they are open to exploring opportunities.

It is important for us to talk to our people and really listen to their experiences. I like to ask my team what causes them frustration in their job. It is important to ask the question and to respond to their responses.

Reflection

- How are you creating a culture where people want to work?
- What are you ignoring or working around?
- What are some ways that you can create a more positive company culture by even 5%?

Chapter 4

The New Company

Joe and Mike went into the new company with an agreement that Joe was going to work for another five years at which time Mike would step in and become the new vice president of sales. That was the deal they had negotiated, and that's what everybody knew. Joe and Mike were very open about it. When the president introduced the hiring of Mike and Joe, she sent an email to the whole organization welcoming them. This was odd. Usually, an announcement like this was reserved for just the vice presidents. *Who was Mike and why was he getting this special email?*

Joe always insisted that Mike attend all executive meetings because he needed to "learn the job." The executive team was not excited about this. At one of the first meetings, the CFO asks, "Why is Mike here? It is not normal to have staff members attend."

"He is learning from me. He goes where I go. How else will we make sure he is in the loop?" Joe remarks.

The CFO fires back, "Haven't you all worked together for years? Doesn't he already know what you expect of him?"

Mike stood up and raised his voice to combat the question. "How does my presence here impact you? Why do you care?'

The CFO thought to himself *what an asshole!*

The president had heard enough. "This was an agreement we made when we hired Joe. He is preparing Mike to be his successor. It is going to be fine."

The CFO then asks, "Can I bring my number 2? I would like to have her in the room."

The president gave him a disapproving look. "We will talk about this later. Let's get down to business."

The executive team quickly noticed from the beginning that Joe and Mike had a tendency to gang up on the rest of the group. They were loud, brash, and dismissive. *Great, how long do we have to deal with this?*

The two also immediately started making changes to the current sales team. They looked at sales numbers and decided who were the top salespeople and who needed to go to bring in fresh ideas and fresh business. The sales team had been together for quite a while. They were not necessarily superstars, but they were getting the job done. They had a reputation for having very strong relationships with their customers, and these customers were the ones that Mike could not sign at his former company. No matter how hard he tried, the clients loved the smaller company and its service. The customers often shared that they could go to a bigger company and have more products, but they liked the people they were working with so much that it didn't make sense to move.

The previous vice president of sales had a philosophy that sales should be about relationship building and not just a transactional process. The team had grown to believe that the more they nurtured and grew their connections, the better the business would be in the long run. In one of the first meetings, Joe told the group, "We have been looking at the numbers, and there is a lot of work to do. We will be having conversations with the low performers." He looked around the room and made eye contact with several of the team. "You all know who you are. We will get you signed up for sales training. Forget all that relationship junk. We need your numbers up now!"

True to their word, Joe and Mike began firing the "low-performing" salespeople. They did not foresee the fallout from these actions, however. When they called the clients to let them know that they would soon have a new company contact, more often than not, the clients were very upset. They told Joe that they had been working with their salespeople for many years, and that relationship was the reason why they stayed with the company. Mike and Joe confidently reassured these clients that they would be well taken care of and that there would be no problems. Unfortunately, they very quickly fell back into their old habits at the new company. Again, they would overpromise and underdeliver.

Within the first year, the company experienced a decline in sales. They had seen many of their long-term customers leave to go to larger companies. The president was distraught and brought together the executives to discuss why. Joe insisted on bringing Mike into this strategy meeting even though the president did not want him there.

"He needs to be part of this solution," Joe defends. "He's got to learn how to navigate this system well before my contract is up."

Mike was the only non-executive in the room. And when other team leaders came into the room, glances of distrust were shot between them. Mike didn't miss a beat, even though he was aware that his presence was unwanted. When questioned about the drop in sales, he explains, "Our team is bringing in sales, but the products team is not delivering the quantity we need to keep our customers satisfied."

The vice president of product services jumped in to defend her team. "You cannot promise what we cannot deliver," she insists. "We are a small company that offers great service, and when you're making big promises, we cannot make that happen."

Mike quickly snaps back. "If you all can't deliver what our customers want, then why are we out there working so hard to make the sale?"

She returns fire. "My team works hard and has amazing client relationships. They are the reason many of our clients stay even when other companies can offer more products. The clients love the service we are able to give them."

"Maybe you all should have less coffee talk with the clients and figure out how to expand what we offer," Mike barks. "You all spend too much time getting to know them. Just give them what they need and move on."

Another leader was sitting in the back of the room just watching Mike's behavior. *What an asshole!*

The meeting continued to escalate, and the president realized the team was divided into two sides——the sales team and everybody else. She had a really important decision to make.

Be the Catalyst

In this chapter, we focus on bad leadership in sales. Bad leadership happens at all levels, jobs, and industries. When we do our own self-reflection, it is easy to think we don't do it or it is someone else. We have to be open to the possibility of our own missteps.

At times as leaders, we think we are doing something positive for our people, but we do the opposite if we don't do it correctly. When we force our ideas on others without building relationships and helping people understand the "why," it can create resentment for all involved. It can also look like special treatment. Mentoring, advising, and coaching are so beneficial as people are moving through their careers. We have to do the right things in the right way.

We can also damage our team when we put them in jobs they are not prepared for and then don't give them the training and support they need to be successful. I have seen it all too often where we promote people because they have "stuck by their side" but they are woefully unqualified. This doesn't mean you don't promote them. Just make sure you're paying attention to their gaps and how you can help them get the skills they need.

Reflection

- Have you ever promoted someone into a position that they were not quite ready for and what were the results?
- How might you set your people up for success?
- What needs to change in your organization to ensure harmonious collaboration between all of your teams?

Chapter 5

The Big Decision

After the meeting, the president knew that they had to make a change but wasn't sure what the change should be, so she pulled in her closest advisers who worked outside of the company. She called her executive coach and walked her through the meeting and explained the animosity in the room.

"I also cannot keep this up. I'm just not sleeping!" Exhaustion echoed in her voice.

"First, remember that you're a great leader, and you have dealt with much harder things than an arrogant sales guy," her coach reminds her.

She knew her coach was right, but she was so tired of having this fight time and time again with bad managers.

The coach continues, "What are your options?"

"The worst part is I know Mike is not an asshole. He is a really great guy, but he really behaves like one sometimes. Joe, on the other hand, I am not sure he cares how others see him." She knew what she had to do.

"I can let the bad behavior continue, and I can lose really great people, or I can talk to Joe and Mike. If I do that, they might leave. This is risky because they are good salespeople. They bring us lots of business," the president explains.

"Just because they can make a sale, are they in line with your company values? Are they behaving in a way that you are proud of for your company?" asks the coach.

"Ugh, no, not at all. It is like they know our values and do the exact opposite. We have even had to stop having them represent us at outside events because of some of their behaviors."

The coach was curious. "What do they do?"

"They were always the loud, crazy ones at the events. Some saw them as the life of the party, and other people were not impressed. That is not who we are," the president shares.

The coach challenges her. "Now is the time for you to show your people that you're a strong leader and can make tough decisions. Believe in yourself and remember why you're in this position. What advice would you give someone facing the same challenges?"

"You're right. I would tell them to be strong, step up, and do their job! Most importantly, to not doubt themselves. I know what I have to do." The president sighs. Difficult conversations, while necessary, were not a favorite of hers.

The following week, the behaviors continued, and the anxiety at work reached new heights. It was like a time bomb waiting to explode. The president decided she would ask Joe to retire early. Joe was responsible for the bad behaviors on his team. He had allowed it to continue, and she knew that he was already planning to retire. *So, what would it hurt?* It was best to part ways and start as fresh as possible.

On Monday morning, the president asked Joe to come into her office. When Joe arrived, she explained that they were going to make a change.

"Joe, we're going to have to modify our agreement," she began. "Members of the team and I have witnessed that you just cannot get along with the rest of the executive team. It is not a good fit, and it's creating a toxic environment."

Joe grew red in the face and stood up. "They just don't know how to work with the sales team," he shouts. "We're making sales. We're doing our job!"

"Everything is not about the sales. If we have a toxic environment and people cannot get along, it is not worth the sales."

"If you don't have sales, you can't pay your bills. How do you not know that?"

"I am not going to argue with you," she explains. "We need to go in a different direction. I don't want it to end this way, but I am not sure I have any other option."

Joe stormed out of her office. "This is going to cost you!" He shouts as he slams the door.

They finally agreed on a separation agreement over three very long weeks of negotiations. The president decided to spin the change as a really exciting announcement that Joe was going to leave the organization to spend more time with his family. They praised Joe at meetings. They celebrated him with a big lunch and gave him a new set of golf clubs on his last day of work. The president thought that everyone was very supportive of the decision, but she did not realize in the back of the room, many people were rolling their eyes, disgusted that he was going out as a hero. Even more frustrating was that Mike was being promoted to his position. What people did not know was that Joe negotiated both in his original hiring and in his separation agreements that Mike would become the new VP.

On Mike's first day as a vice president of sales, the president brought him into her office and explained to him that they had to see changes in the position. He was tasked with making sure that the sales team could work with the other departments in the organization. As he prepared to leave, she adds, "And Mike, you will be watched closely. I expect a quick turnaround in our sales—and in the office environment."

When Mike left the office, he was torn. He was angry at what happened to his mentor, and he was excited about his new opportunity. However, he was a little puzzled by the challenge of being able to work with everybody else. He had always been told that sales are what runs a company. *Why do I have to bend?*

Mike met with the sales team and let them know that they were going to be working on new goals and new expectations. He was going to be sharing with them the sales tools that he used, and he expected them to be put into play as well.

"I'm also going to set up one-on-one meetings with all of you to regularly review your sales numbers––and you will be pushed."

"I'm here to support you, and I also want you to know what I expect out of you. Let me know if you have questions," he adds.

When the meeting was over, Mike left the room with confidence that he had nailed the meeting. Little did he know the team stayed behind. Everyone chimed in.

"What was that?"

"Are you kidding me?"

"Does he really think we can learn anything from him?"

"Well, maybe he will do a great job."

"We should give him a chance."

"Are you both crazy? You have worked with him, and you know him!"

"He has been an asshole and now he has a title. What is going to change?"

Ninety days into the job, Mike met with the president to review the work they had been doing. Sales were not necessarily getting better, but they were not getting worse.

She let him know that while his performance was OK, his relationships with his peers, the sales numbers, and his leadership needed to continue to improve. He was also expected to develop his team and help them learn! He didn't know what that meant by developing his team. He was teaching them the way he learned. It was working for him. *Why wouldn't it work for them?*

Mike went back to his office to review the sales sheets. He started marking off the high performers, the regular performers, and the low performers. He loved a good competition and decided to hold an office contest. He felt that if he could motivate the team through competition everybody would get their sales up.

Be the Catalyst

As leaders, often we have to do what is right and not what is easy. When we allow bad behavior to continue without accountability, that sends messages to not just the person with the bad behavior but to everyone in the organization. I am a big supporter of coaching to success. Our people can't grow if they don't know. Being a leader can be hard because you often have to have extremely difficult conversations.

There are lots of great tips and tools out there to become more comfortable with these conversations. I am a big fan of *Crucial Conversations* by Kerry Patterson. I use the model personally and train my leaders to use it as well. You will never enjoy difficult conversations, but you can practice and get better at them!

Reflection

- How are you preventing toxicity from spreading through your culture?
- How are you holding your people accountable?
- What changes might need to happen to ensure a healthy work environment for all?

Chapter 6

The Contest

The next morning Mike was unusually chipper. The team was unsure of what was going on and what to think--especially when he called another meeting. One of the team members asks, "Why are we meeting again? We just met yesterday!"

Mike smiles, "Just come on into the meeting room. I have an exciting announcement."

He glanced around the room as everyone settled into their seats.

"I know you all love a good competition, so we are going to be looking at everyone's sales for the quarter. Those who are in the top five will get a bonus, and those in the bottom 5% will be put on a performance improvement plan," he explains.

There was a mix of shock and excitement in the room. The top performers knew they had this in the bag and would have no issue getting the bonus. Those with lower sales numbers felt panic and started asking questions.

"Are you just looking at the sales numbers, or will you be looking at client retention, client satisfaction, or anything else?" a team member asks.

"No, it is just about the sales goals. We have to make some money," Mike adds.

He then rolled out a giant whiteboard with everybody's goals noted. He also included their historical data of where they had met their goals and where they had not.

After the meeting, he pulled his top two salespeople—one male and one female, aside. He shared an idea he had about the bottom two salespeople. "Let's take this game up a level. All of the times that the bottom two salespeople either make a bad decision, ask a stupid question, or just leave a deal on the table, we will track it," he suggests. With a look of glee in his eyes, he opened his closet door and had a small whiteboard there with two stick figures—one was a man, and one was a woman. He did not write the name of the bottom two performers, but the two top salespeople knew who they were. They were both all in on this idea.

Throughout the quarter, the top salespeople would come into Mike's office, not say anything, pick up a marker, open the closet door, and put a mark on one of the two stick figures. Chuckling, they'd then walk out of the room. They would do this no matter what was going on. If Mike's door was closed, they would quietly come in and make their marks. The way the closet door opened Mike could see what they were doing but the person sitting on the other side of the desk could not. If someone asked what was happening, Mike would tell them they were tracking sales data.

One time, Mike was in a meeting with the president of the company in his office, and one of the top salespeople walked in, grabbed a marker, made a mark, and walked out.

"What's that about?" she asks with concern rising in her voice. *How dare someone just come into the office without knocking or checking to make sure it is ok?*

She stood up and opened the closet door to find the whiteboard, stick figures, and markings.

"What is this?" she asks.

Mike laughs. "It is no big deal."

She presses him for an explanation. "Who are the stick figures, and what are the markings?"

"We're just having some fun with the team." He tries to dodge the interrogation.

She was getting more agitated. "Who are the stick figures?"

Mike finally gave in. "They are low performers. I was just trying to find ways to push everyone to meet their sales goals. And those two," he points to the stick figures. "They have no clue what we're doing. We're not hurting their feelings."

She was shocked. "This is nonsense. You need to stop this immediately."

"Do you have something against us having some fun?" he quips. "We work really hard around here to meet our quotas. No one is being harmed, and it is just an innocent joke."

With a stern glance, the president turned to leave the office, pausing at the doorway. "This will stop or there will be consequences," she warns.

Mike summoned his team of high performers into his office and explained that the president was upset. "We've got to be much more low-key about this game," he explains. He made new rules. "No one should come into the office when the door is closed, or someone is here. And you need to keep your tally marks to yourselves. We'll meet and tally together," he says as he stood up to erase the whiteboard. "Get your notes before this disappears." They quickly took out their notepads to record what was on the whiteboard before he erased it.

The quarter ended, and the team was more divided than ever. The top salespeople were continuing to make their sales and growing their sales numbers. The rest of the group felt unsupported, and those newer to the profession, newer to the company, or just younger in their experience, were not getting any help from the more experienced salespeople. In the past, the team really worked cohesively, supporting each other, and even sharing referrals. Not anymore. It was now every man and woman for themselves!

The week before the end of the quarter, the president brought Mike into her office for a regular check-in meeting. "How are things going?"

Mike was confident in his answer. "We are making progress. Those who I knew would get it done are getting it done. I told you we had some dead weight."

"Mike, come on. You can do better than this. We have talked about it. Are you supporting the team and giving them training?"

Mike pushes back. "I gave them what I had." He then left the office more frustrated than ever.

When the president saw the sales numbers at the end of the quarter, she became even more concerned. *Why was there this big divide that never existed before? Did it have to do with the stick figures that were in Mike's office? What was going on in the sales team?*

Be the Catalyst

Psychological safety is a belief that people won't be punished or humiliated for speaking up. It is safe to share ideas, ask questions, raise concerns, and make mistakes. It also focuses on the importance of being one team and not having an in-crowd and out-crowd.

Amy Edmondson discovered the importance of psychological safety in her doctoral research. She shares that it is "a key factor in healthy teams." Her book *The Fearless Organization* is a great read as well as her TED Talks.

Reflection

- How are you creating a safe environment for everyone on your team?
- What extra training might be called for if team members are faltering?
- How are you creating the essence of everyone playing on the same team?

Chapter 7

A Difficult Conversation

The president brought Mike into the office to ask him about the disparity in sales numbers. Mike explains, "As I told you, there are some of the salespeople that work harder than others, and those people took my challenge seriously."

She was so frustrated. "Does this have anything to do with the stick figures in your office? I did tell you to stop doing it."

"We erased it as soon as you requested." He left out the part that they were still tracking the stick figures.

The president adds, "I'm in an uncomfortable position, much like I was with Joe. I'm concerned about your effect on the team."

She looked at him pointedly and then explained that he needed to do some reflection on himself as a leader. "Mike, I am not sure you are happy here. And I'd like you to consider a few questions I have of you: Are you in the right place? Do you have the skills you need to do the job? Are you a leader?" She told him they would meet later in the week to discuss it further.

Mike left the office, and he was angry. *How dare she!* He had worked so hard on the new incentives, the new goals, and his top salespeople. *How could he be to blame because the bottom people didn't know how to do their jobs?*

The president was so disappointed when he left. *Why is he acting like an asshole? Can he change?*

Later that night, he went out with some friends at a local pub. He wasn't sure he wanted to go out but also was really not sure of anything now. Mike shared about how hard he had worked to build his team and that the company was ungrateful. "I am so sick of building strong sales teams and then companies just can't get their acts together," he vents. No one said anything so he continues. "Sales is not easy, and to have to keep jumping is exhausting. I can't keep building up my new client base."

Mike believed the company did not understand who he was and that they did not value him. His friend, Julie, suggested that maybe he needed to look for a change and find a new company. "If I leave the company, they are going to have me on a non-compete which will limit my options for finding another job here. This is all I know! I have never been in a different industry or job."

As the rest of the group was talking more about their workday, he realized he was the only one who was truly unhappy. Everyone else had stress and things going on, but nobody was as unhappy as he was.

Later in the evening, he asked Julie about her company and her job, and she explained that they had fantastic leadership.

"It is a great company. I have been there since college and can't imagine working anywhere else."

Mike was intrigued by this. "What makes it so special?"

"I just really feel like I belong there. I am important to them. We are able to approach the executive team with our ideas and share ways that the company could be better," she explains. "We really like each other and enjoy spending time together——inside and outside of the office."

"Really!" Mike responds with surprise. "I never socialize with the people I work with. The less they know about me, the better——and vice versa."

"That doesn't sound like much fun," she adds. She pauses and sips her drink. "The executive team also trusts us. I find that as long as I'm doing my job, I am pretty much left alone unless I needed help."

Mike laughs. "I'm sure the company is not very profitable. Sounds pretty fluffy to me! Do you guys have pizza parties on Friday as well?"

"We do have pizza parties to celebrate our success," she says. "Plus, every time the financials come out, and we are not just meeting goals, but we have been exceeding them——as a team, we're rewarded with bonuses."

Mike did not believe her. *No one loves their job like that. Right? It is called work for a reason.* Mike got quiet again. He did not want to leave, but he also did not want to go home and be alone. Instead, he listened to everyone's stories, continuing to marvel how for the most part everyone was satisfied with their jobs and enjoyed the people they worked with.

For the rest of the night, they all talked about their dating life, families, and social activities they were involved in. Several of them were talking about their volunteer work and the boards they served on. Mike thought to himself, "*Here we go again, more fluff! Where do these people get all this energy?*"

The night out did not help his unhappiness. It actually made him feel worse. He went home and tried to sleep. He just kept tossing and turning. *Is this how life is supposed to be?* Mike was so disappointed and frustrated. *Why was this happening? I have worked hard and deserve better!*

The following Sunday, he went to his parent's house as he always did for family dinner. His sisters and their partners were also there. He usually looked forward to family time, but this night was an exception. He did not want to be there.

The dinner was exactly how he expected it to go. Lots of conversations about work. His sisters were all doing great in their jobs. They were so happy. And on that night, his youngest sister had a big announcement. "We are getting married."

Everyone at the table was so excited. Lots of cheers and toasts from everyone. His middle sister was not drinking during the toasts. Mike thought to himself, "*What is that all about?*"

Before he could ask, she chimes in. "I don't want to steal anyone's big night, but I can't wait to share. She grabbed her husband's hand and made the announcement her parents had been waiting to hear, "We are pregnant." More cheers from everyone. Now Mike's mother was crying tears of joy.

"What a night!" His dad adds. "Mike, do you have anything to share?"

Here we go again. Why won't they accept I am not in a hurry to get married and have children?

At this point, Mike realized everyone was waiting on his answer. He just shook his head and went back to eating. He could not get out of the house soon enough. He wanted to be happy for his sisters, but he also did not need this pressure.

As he was leaving for the night, his mom pulled him aside. "What is going on? Are you ok?"

Mike and his mom had a special relationship. He knew he could tell her anything. "I am just not happy. Work sucks, and I might get fired."

She knew something was wrong but not this bad. "What in the world is going on? What have you done?" While she loved Mike, she also knew he was not perfect.

Mike knew his mom held him to a high standard and also knew that she loved him. He valued her opinion. He then described the last few months at work. He did leave out some details of the stick figures, and anything else he felt might disappoint his mother. He hated disappointing her.

She quickly hugged him and told him everything would be ok. She encouraged him to listen to the president and see if he could find a way to make it work. Mike assured her he would do what he could and then left to get some rest before the big conversation tomorrow.

Be the Catalyst

Honest and kind conversations are so important. It is not always easy to hear the truth but it is so important. How can we know the impact we are having on people if people are not honest with us?

Too often we are afraid of hurting someone's feelings so instead of telling them the truth we beat around the bush or avoid it at all costs. When we are unclear, we are really doing our people a disservice. How can we expect people to improve and get better if they don't know what they need to be working on? It is not always easy to hear the truth, but it is important.

Reflection

- How are you impacting those around you?
- How might you be more honest with yourself––and others?
- Do you allow others to be honest with you?

Chapter 8

The Final Conversation

At the end of the week, Mike went into the office knowing that he had to meet with the president later that day. He was still uneasy and more frustrated than when he last spoke to the president. He had not slept the night before and was anxious about the conversation. He'd never been fired, and quite frankly, he had never experienced not being successful. *Why was she not supporting him and his success?*

When they sat down in the meeting together, the president quickly asked Mike if he had thought about the previous conversations.

"Yes, I have," he replies sheepishly. "I also spoke with my mom and several friends about what we had discussed."

He pauses and looks her straight in the eye. "I was really surprised by your comments because I have always met my sales goals, and while some members of the team are struggling, the rest of them are getting things done. It was really about cutting the dead weight rather than about whether I'm a good leader or not."

"I disagree," she says, leaning forward and putting her elbows on the desk. "We're trying to change the culture. There's a problem that's been occurring. We're experiencing high turnover throughout the organization and profits are decreasing."

Mike nods.

She continues, "Let's talk about the questions I asked you to think about. First, do you think you are in the right place? Do you want to work here?"

"I don't know. I like everyone, enough. From the conversations I have had with my friends, they are all so happy at work. I just have not been able to fully connect with anyone. I don't know why. I want to be happy here," he offers.

"I know it is hard, and I was so hopeful without Joe you would be able to succeed," she explains. "Do you feel you have the right skills to do the job?"

"I am doing what I know. I have only worked for Joe," he shares. "I am a good salesperson. I am always the top in sales. What other skills do I need to be a salesperson?"

"You're a vice president. You need to be a leader. I need you to be able to build a strong team, make connections, and create an environment where everyone feels comfortable. Do you think you're doing that, acting like a good leader?" she challenges.

"Well, I am trying." His response was filled with exasperation.

"You make good sales, but you were moved up to be in a leadership position, and you manage people now," the president adds. "You can't just be good at sales. You need to be able to teach others how to be good at their jobs and be a leader. I need you to step up and do that."

Mike again was showing signs of frustration. "I don't even know what that means."

The president pauses, reflecting upon her next remark.

"Mike, I am so sorry! I made a mistake, and I did not give you what you need to be successful. I did not set you up for success. I wish I could fix this, but I think the damage is so big that it is irreparable," she responds. "We need to make a change to ensure that sales goals are met, we retain our clients, and we build good relationships with their internal customers."

Now Mike was furious. "Are you kidding me? You promote me, don't train me, don't give me clear directions, then you want to let me go?"

Mike's face now grew red with anger, but beneath that was another level of worry. He knew from his earlier reflection that he had burned many bridges in the industry because he was known as a cutthroat and get-it-done-at-all-cost type of person! *What am I going to do? I am 36! Is that too old or not old enough? I am in the middle stage of my career and don't know where to go!*

"Please give me one more chance," he begs. "I know I can do better and build a successful team."

"How will you do better, Mike? What are the steps you will take?" she prods.

Mike was trying to get himself under control but also wanted to push her for help. "I don't know yet, but I will figure it out, especially if I get some guidance from you. Plus, I have always been able to figure it out!"

The president was caught between a rock and a hard place. She held a great deal of compassion for Mike—and at the same time, had responsibility for the company as a whole. "Mike, you don't have any good answers. You don't even know where to start. We are in such bad financial shape. I don't have time to train you on how to be a leader. I need someone to lead our sales team that already knows how to lead."

This is where the president had to have the most difficult conversations of her career. She wanted to help him grow, but as an executive, she could not allow the egregious behavior to continue.

"Mike, whether intentionally or unintentionally, you have created a toxic culture. You have alienated the rest of the executive team and your sales team has lost confidence in you."

Mike knew what was coming, and he could not look her in the eye. "Just say it."

She continues to explain. "This is not all about you. It is about the organization as a whole. You and Joe did great damage to the culture with your cutthroat behaviors. You have damaged relationships inside and outside of the organization. There is no way I can save you."

Mike stood up, ready to have this done. "Are you going to just say it?"

She stood up as well. "Mike, I want you to be happy and you are not happy here. Let me help you find something. You get a fresh start and so do we."

As he storms out, he says angrily, "No, thank you. You have done enough."

Later that day, he was sitting in HR still stunned. It was all a blur. He could hear the HR director talking but could not comprehend what he was saying. When it got quiet, Mike looked up and hear the HR director say, "I wish you all the best. Here is all your paperwork. Review with your attorney and call me if you have any questions."

Mike nodded, grabbed the papers, and walked out. *My attorney! I don't have an attorney. I don't even know what just happened.* When he got to the parking lot, he stared at his severance agreement. It was not a bad dream. This was happening.

Be the Catalyst

As we move through our career journey, we have more and more responsibilities to the organization as a whole. If we don't take that into account when making decisions, we run the risk of having negative impacts. When we allow bad behavior to continue, it has a drastic impact on the bottom line. Organizations with a toxic culture experience higher turnover and lower productivity.

Much research has been done on the impact of culture on an organization. Deloitte Consulting LLP released findings that stated organizations that proactively manage culture demonstrate a 516% growth over a 10-year period. Those that don't focus on culture have higher turnover, lower workplace satisfaction and ultimately lower profits.

Reflection

- Where do your expectations and actions not align?
- How would you rate the health of your company's culture?
- What are you doing well and what needs improvement?

Chapter 9

What Now?

Mike was devastated. Sales were all he knew. Then the real panic set in. *How am I going to pay my bills? Where will I go? Do I have to move cities? I don't have a business network anymore!*

Mike wanted to go home, be alone, and not think about any of this. Maybe if he just ignored it, it would all go away. He knew that was not the answer, but he really did not have any answers at this point.

On Sunday, when he did not show up to family dinner his mom called. "Mike, are you ok? We are all worried about you. Are you not coming to dinner?" she asks.

Mike never missed dinner, but he couldn't face everyone. "Mom, I was fired." As he said the words, he realized he had not said them out loud, and he started to cry. At first, it was a faint whimper, and then he could not control it. All the emotions came flooding out of him.

His mom felt helpless. "I am coming over. Can I bring you dinner?"

Mike was shaking his head as if she could see him. "No, Mom, I will be ok. I will call you later this week."

He spent the majority of the week feeling sorry for himself. He did not leave his house and was not answering calls from his family.

On Thursday, his mom showed up at his house. He did not want to let her in but also knew she was not going to stop knocking until he opened the door. "Mom, I am fine. It will be fine."

"You're not fine. I get that you feel bad, but it is time to dust yourself off," she shares. "You can't sit here and feel sorry for yourself. Learn from this and let's move on."

Mike wanted to fight her on this, but he knew she was right. She was usually right. She knew him well and wanted what was best for him.

Later that day, he sent a message to his friend, Julie, to ask if they could have coffee.

"Julie, I would like to catch up and talk about work. I know you said you liked your company, and I was wondering if you all had any openings," he wrote.

Julie quickly responded. "I am always happy to join you for coffee and to talk about the amazing company and my great coworkers." She was so proud and happy at work.

A few days later, they met at a little local coffee shop. It was busy but after they ordered their drinks, they found a comfy seating area in the back corner.

Julie knew something was wrong but wasn't sure what was going on. "How are you, Mike?"

Mike was still very distraught. "I was fired last week. They didn't even give me a chance to do anything differently," he announces. "They really did me wrong. I was doing the best I could, but nobody was helping me out. Now I am trying to figure out my next steps. I need a job!"

"I am so sorry. That has to be so difficult. I encourage you to do some soul-searching and don't just accept any position. You won't be happy if it is not a fit."

"I get it, but I have to pay my bills. I am too old for this. I have worked too hard. I really don't even know what I would do. I need a company that will help me grow, but I don't even know what that means. I'm just so unsure about what to do." He stared out over the crowd looking very forlorn.

"There are great companies out there that will help you figure it out." She told him that her company had coaching and training programs from the beginning to the end whether you were starting your career or getting ready to retire. They were always investing in their people. Career conversations were standard practice about the next steps, and then the company leadership would map out training programs to help team members reach goals.

"Our company does more than look for a cultural fit when hiring," she explains. "The leaders want everyone to feel like they belong in the organization. We do a lot of work on inclusion and belonging. Those are part of the company's core values! If any employee made anyone feel like they did not belong at the organization, there were consequences if the behavior was not adjusted."

"What does that even look like?" Mike asks, thoroughly confused.

Julie takes a deep breath and studies Mike. She learned from her company that it is important to have kind but at times difficult conversations rather than just being nice. If we are not honest with people, they cannot grow. "Mike, this is not going to be easy to say but it is important for me to tell you the truth. I am telling you this because I care about you. There are some openings, but well below the level that you've worked before," she says. "I'm hesitant to recommend you, though because of the way your last job ended."

One of the values that her organization had was to be a humble leader and to practice humility no matter what your position in the organization. "I don't think you're humble," she adds. "You'll probably end up failing with our organization as well."

Mike was hurt and a bit stunned. Then, he took a deep breath. He had tried to brace himself when she told him it was going to be hard to hear. "That hurts but I appreciate the feedback," he replies. "I need to think about this some more."

"Let me know how I can help," she adds. "I really want the best for you."

He called his mother as he drove home to share the conversation that he had with Julie. "I am interested in the company that Julie works for, and I really think I can do a good job."

His mom asks, "Do you understand why Julie is hesitant to recommend you?"

"No, Mom! I have worked hard in my career, and it is not my problem that my previous boss did not see it that way."

"You have now been told twice that you are not humble," she adds. "Maybe there's something to it. Maybe you should think about it and figure out a way to improve in those areas. I am not saying you're an asshole, you just might be behaving like one."

Her response was not what he wanted to hear but probably what he needed to hear.

Mike was sad, hurt, and even more confused. Now his mom was confirming what others were saying to him. *Am I too old to start over?*

Be the Catalyst

Who we are and how we show up at work impacts those around us. It is important for organizations to have people on the team that want to grow themselves and others.

Patrick Lencioni talks about being humble, hungry, and smart in his book *The Ideal Team Player*. He explains that those who are humble admit their mistakes, share credit with their team, and acknowledge their weaknesses. "Hungry" individuals are passionate about the team, feel a personal responsibility for the team's overall success, and look for opportunities to contribute. Smart is defined as those who show empathy to others, listen to all on the team, and are aware of how their actions impact others.

When we hire people for their competencies and values fit, more often than not, we can train them for the job. I recommend focusing less on tasks and more on competencies. Let's look at what our people need to exhibit to do the job.

Reflection

- How are you putting the right people in place to build strong teams?
- How are you taking responsibility for the team's overall success?
- How are you humble, hungry, and smart?

Chapter 10

Am I An Asshole?

Every morning for the next few weeks, Mike woke up and then went back to bed or moved to the couch. He didn't have the courage to face the truth.

What Julie said to him just kept echoing in his head. He always was a success, so how could anyone not think that he was a good person? He had clients that stayed with him in the different companies that he had worked for, and he had people whom he still spoke to from the other companies. *Why do I have a reputation around town for not being a good guy? And more importantly, why didn't anyone tell me until now?*

The next month, Mike called Julie. He needed to continue their conversation. "Julie, how have you been?"

Julie was happy to hear from Mike. He had not responded when she texted. "I am great. We have all missed seeing you at happy hour. How are you?"

Mike was not sure if he should fake it or if he should just be honest. *What do I have to lose?* "Not really great. Still trying to decide on the next steps. I can't stop thinking about what you told me when we had coffee."

Julie quickly responds. "I am so sorry this has been so hard. How can I help you?"

It was odd how much he trusted Julie. They had not been super close before all this happened. *Why was she so kind to him, and, more importantly to him, why did he trust her so much?*

"I would love to have lunch," he says. "I have not left my house lately and have not seen a lot of people. I could use socialization."

Julie could not wait to hear what Mike was thinking about his next steps. They met at the little local pub that was right around the corner from her office. It was the place their friends also met for happy hour during the week and to watch games on the weekend.

After some quick pleasantries, they jumped right in. "I just couldn't get over what you said to me about the type of person I am at work," he confesses.

"When you're not working, you're a great guy who is so fun to be around and generous with your friends," she says.

Mike really enjoyed hearing this. It made him feel a bit better.

"But," Julie continues, "Your reputation in the workplace is that you run over those around you to get your way and meet your goals. This is a little, big town. People talk."

Mike thought, *Ugh, here we go again!* "I understand, and I really want to do better. I don't want people to not want to work with me," he confesses. "I think it is also damaging my relationships outside of work."

"I don't think you are intentionally being an asshole, but I do believe currently you're not the type of person anyone wants to be around anyplace," she replies.

Mike nods. "I want to work on that, but to be honest, I don't know what my next steps are."

Julie felt Mike was sincere and really wanted to help him. "Okay, there's an opening at the company. I'll talk with leadership and see what they think," she says.

They enjoyed the rest of their lunch, and as they walked out, several people from Julie's office passed by. They were chatting and laughing. They quickly noticed Julie and gave her big hugs. As she and Mike said goodbye, Julie promised to be in touch soon. She also made him promise he would show up for their next happy hour with their friends. "You know none of us are judging you. We want you to be happy and successful. We are only telling you these things because we care about you," she shares.

"I know, and I am trying to not just hear you but to really listen. It doesn't make it easier to hear, but at least you all are being honest with me," he adds.

Later that day, Julie was talking to her boss, Allison, and shared the conversation that she had with Mike.

"I heard you had lunch at the pub today. I had a meeting so missed it when the group went over," Allison says.

"I was wondering where you were when they walked in," Julie says. "I wanted to introduce you to Mike. I think you would really like him."

Allison was very interested to hear about Mike's backstory and his revelation over the last month. Allison loved to work with people like this because someone took a chance on her to grow her as a leader earlier in her career. And now, Allison was a great leader. She was open, flexible, and she loved to watch other people succeed. Allison also knew she had made some really bad mistakes that led her to have a messy path to leadership. It was early on in her career that one of her bosses pulled her into his office and said to her, "You have so much potential, but you need to understand that you're not the most important person in the room."

Allison was thinking about this conversation and her own career journey. That was probably one of the single most important things that anyone had said to her. Early in her career, she was very hard-driving and very accomplished, and every time people talked behind closed doors, she always felt like the question was, *What are they saying about me?* When her boss chided her that not everything was about her, she began to understand the complex nature of running an organization. She realized she had to stop worrying about what others were saying about her, focus on her responsibilities, and do the best job possible.

After Julie shared Mike's story, Allison told her she was thinking about the next steps. She would probably want to meet with him, but she wanted to mull it over a little. When Julie left, Allison was excited and curious. She had seen situations like this go two different ways. There were the people who said they wanted to improve but really didn't want to do the hard work it took——and then those who were willing to be vulnerable. The journey was not going to be easy, but if done correctly, Mike could definitely become a strong leader.

Be the Catalyst

Being a good leader is more than just checking tasks off your checklist. It is about creating relationships with your team and helping them grow. GLINT and LinkedIn Learning released a "The 2021 State of the Manager" report that emphasized the importance of strong leadership. They reported that employees who find their managers inspirational are two times more likely to feel optimistic about their own happiness at work. Employees also reported that those who are inspired by their managers are twice as likely to be engaged, stay with their organization, and be more likely to have clarity about their organization.

As we grow in our careers, it is important to surround ourselves with people who will help us grow. A strong advisory group, coach, or mentor is beneficial. An advisory group is a person or group you can discuss your professional growth with. They are open and honest with you. They don't just tell you what you want to hear.

Reflection

- How are your employees inspired by you?
- How do you create relationships with your team members?
- Who is in your advisory group? And if you don't have one, who would you like to enlist?

Chapter 11

A Second Chance

The first thing the next morning in the office Allison stopped by Julie's desk. "I thought a lot about our conversation, and I would love to meet Mike. Can you set up coffee for us?"

"Of course!" Julie offers. "He is a bit nervous because I told him I shared his whole story with you."

"Tell him not to worry," Allison says. "I love to help people open to a second chance, but he has to be open to the conversations."

Julie quickly called Mike to set up the coffee. "Allison would love to meet you. I told her you're nervous. But when you meet with her, you need to be open and authentic. Don't overthink it."

Mike was excited about the coffee but also hesitant. *What will she think of me? Can I do this? What am I doing?* Mike did everything to talk himself out of the coffee meeting. The day before the meeting he started a text to Julie to cancel. That was the point when he had another hard conversation with himself. *What are you doing? Stop doubting yourself. You can't live like this!*

As he walked into the coffee shop, he arrived early to get a coffee and find a seat. He also knew that he had to get there early to relax and focus. When Allison walked in, she looked around, and they made eye contact. Mike introduced himself quickly and nervously.

"I've been eager to meet you," Allison says. "I understand you've had a rough few weeks."

Mike's nerves got the best of him, and he jumped right in. "It has been difficult, but I realized there was some truth to what people were saying."

"It is not easy to hear the truth, but it can be the best gift you receive," Allison shares. "I have made some big mistakes throughout my career, and if people had not been kind to me nor given me grace, I don't know where I would be. It was hard to hear from people that at times I was viewed as an asshole. I did not want to be I just did not know better."

Mike reflects for a few seconds. "Would you help me understand your journey and how you made the change?" he asks. "Julie alluded to some challenges you had but never told me the stories."

"Of course. It's not pretty, but it is important because it is what got me to where I am today. I happily share my story so people know that they can make mistakes and can do better," she adds.

Mike was pretty much obsessed at this point to get started. He wanted to be successful, but more importantly, he wanted people to like him. He just couldn't get over the fact that no one in his life had ever told him that he was being an asshole. Nobody said that they didn't want to work with him. When people left the organization, they would always say that it was for more money or more opportunity. They never told him that it was because of his leadership. *Why didn't anyone tell me?* That then led him to wonder if he would have even listened to them if they told them. *Did people tell me, and I just didn't listen?*

He was eager to understand what he missed. *What were the red flags that I haven't paid attention to?*

He confessed all of the things he was feeling to Allison. He was very open about his success in high school and college, his first job, and how he was one of the youngest people to become a vice president of sales at his last company. He told her all about Joe and how Joe was so supportive of him and invited him into meetings that he shouldn't have been in but Joe insisted because he was such a high performer.

Allison listened intently and also remembered early in her career how familiar this sounded. She had made many of these mistakes. She knew that Mike needed to hear that she had been fired not once, but twice because she was being less than humble in her career journey. Every time she would get in trouble at work and was fired, she would blame somebody else. *Well, it's their loss! I am the best they ever had.* It took her quite a while to see the big picture and understand the thing that was holding her back was her!

Throughout the coffee, Allison shared with Mike her journey, her missteps, her successes, and what turned her around. She says, "People always liked me, and I thought I was able to build relationships."

Early in her career, she was always given big projects and was known as the go-to person. "I would work late and come in early to make sure everyone knew how committed I was," she adds. "I worked weekends and would respond to emails immediately. I wanted people to know I was all in all the time. So intense!"

Mike nodded because he had been in that same spot.

"I thought I was on the quick track to success and that nothing could slow me down," Allison confesses. "I did not fully understand that I didn't make deep connections and that I was not building strong teams...until I met John."

John changed her career track. She met John at a networking event. He was a highly successful CEO of one of the top companies in town. He was also very open and giving and supportive of everyone in the room. Everyone liked John, and everyone knew who he was.

Allison was sure that John would be her ticket to the next step in her career. He was well-connected and had strong relationships in town. If he vouched for you almost anywhere, he could open that door for you. Little did she know what was ahead of her.

She asked John if they could have coffee to learn about him and share a little bit about her career journey. John accepted.

When they met later that week, Allison learned more about John's life and his career path. As she pressed him for more of his life stories, he turned his attention to her. "I want to hear about what you're doing. How are things going for you?"

"I am overwhelmed and not sure I am working to my full potential. And I am working all the time. Early in my career, I was getting all the big projects but lately, I feel like I have been put in time-out. I am not getting invited to be involved like I used to."

"What changed? Do you know?" he inquires.

"I really don't know. I got a promotion and was leading a team of four. I had been a supervisor but never been the boss per se. It has been a bit overwhelming. I have always thought I build strong relationships but boy was I wrong. I am not sure my people like me," Allison says.

John had smiled which annoyed Allison. *Is he laughing at me?* "This is normal. Too often companies promote people to leadership roles and don't give them training on how to lead people," he says. "I am happy to share with you my experiences if you are interested in doing the work."

Very quickly Allison agreed, and they set up meetings every four weeks to talk about her career journey. The focus of their meetings was on what was going well and what she needed to work on. John made it clear that she had work to do. Building leadership skills can be challenging. It takes self-awareness, and at times, leaning into being uncomfortable in order to grow. To become a stronger leader, she had to be willing to do some self-assessments and be open to hearing other people's feedback. She shared with Mike that this fateful meeting with John changed her whole career path!

Mike wanted to hear more but Allison had to run to another meeting. He didn't realize they had been there for almost two hours. They scheduled another meeting, and Allison promised she would share more of her journey and about John.

Be the Catalyst

I encourage leaders to write a personal leadership philosophy. This is where you take your values and turn them into a statement as to the type of leader you want to be. Everyone has their own leadership philosophies on how to work with people and what to share. Remember, not all of your people will be looking for the same level of openness. As leaders, it is our responsibility to understand what our people need and how we can provide it to them. We want to be authentic but also support our people at the level they need. Everyone is an individual, so taking the time to build a trusting relationship will help you lead.

Reflection

- How are you being authentic at work?
- What prevents you from being seen and heard for who you are?
- What is one small way you can be more open?

Chapter 12

The Reset

After leaving coffee with Allison, Mike was already counting down the days until they could meet again. He knew Allison was busy, and he really appreciated her time. More importantly, he valued how open she was with him. Frequently, leaders don't share all the dirty details of their career journey. When you look at social media or hear people at parties, so many of them appear to have the "perfect" life.

As a result, Sunday dinner with his family had a different feel. His mother recognized it before he sat down at the table. "You seem chipper. I'm happy to see that. What's going on?"

Mike smiles. "I had a great lunch with my friend, Julie. She agreed to share my story with her boss, Allison, who Julie said had a similar story to mine." He pauses. "And when I met Allison for coffee, she was very open about her career path, which had its share of ups and downs."

"Wow, one coffee changes everything?" Mom remarks.

Mike frowns. "No, Mom. It's not about the coffee. It is more about knowing I'm not alone. Other people have had a rough road and found success on the other side. I might be acting like an asshole, but I can do better."

His mom gave him a big hug. As he was about to share more, his youngest sister and her fiancé came into the house. Before they could close the door, his other sisters came in as well with their partners.

Everyone was so happy to see him. He had not been to dinner in over a month. There were a lot of updates he had missed, and they wanted to hear about his career search. Mike was still a bit uneasy about the career talk with the family. He was not quite ready for that conversation. He wanted to hear about the other family news.

After dinner, on his drive home, he felt so rejuvenated. He had missed his family time so much and hadn't realized how much he needed them—and his friends. He pulled over and texted some of his friends to see if they were still at the corner pub watching the Sunday night football game. Julie quickly sent a note back. "It is just halftime. Come on down. Plenty of game left."

When he walked in, the group was sitting at their regular table. It had been way too long since he had joined them. Everyone quickly welcomed him with hugs and handshakes. For the first time in a long time, he was feeling normal. He'd had a great dinner with his family, and now he was out with his friends.

Julie moved over to the bench to give him a spot to sit. "We are glad you're back. How is everything going?"

Mike felt the genuineness in her statement. "I am doing well. I had a great coffee meeting with Allison. She is amazing."

Julie could not help but smile. "I told you how great she was. The best part about her is she is so authentic and willing to admit when she's made mistakes or circumstances with the company might not be the best they could be. That sounds weird to say about a boss, but it makes me feel like I don't have to be perfect either."

Mike totally understood what Julie was talking about. He had worked with too many people over the years that always had to portray themselves as perfect. "I worked with an operations director who was the worst," he shares. "I am not sure if she was lying to herself or lying to us. Anytime anything went wrong or a hint of an issue, she would double down on how great everything was and how things weren't so bad. She was such an asshole. But she did not care!"

Julie knew exactly that type of person.

Mike continues, "I wondered if she rode a unicorn to work each day. What world was she living in? We were having severe financial issues as an organization, and turnover was high. We would be sitting in executive team meetings, and she was always trying to tell everyone that everything was going to be ok. It is fine."

Julie laughs and nods. "Oh yes, I have totally worked for that type of person. They would never admit their mistakes or even hold people accountable because they did not like conflict."

Mike was having fun with the storytelling but also had a tinge in his gut, *could someone be saying this stuff about me? YIKES! I was not the best leader.*

That is when Mike turned it on himself. "Oh boy, I can only imagine the stories people say about me. There was the time I was promoted to vice president, and before the emails went out, I was parked in the VP parking spot. Looking back now, I felt so entitled. Who cares about a parking spot?"

Julie cringed a little at his admission. She knew there are many people out there that work for the title and the stuff that comes with it. "That is a tough look, Mike. What an asshole!"

They both laugh. "Yes, it was," Julie adds. "There are two types of leaders. The type that works for the title and the type that works for the people. Managers typically fall under that first type. They aren't leading anyone anywhere. I can't follow that type of person."

Mike nods. Another great nugget from Julie. When the game was over, he did not want to leave but he also knew he had to get to work on the next chapter in his journey. Tomorrow was a new day.

When Mike woke up on Monday, for the first time in a very long time, he felt so energized. He had work to do on himself, and he was ready to get started.

Be the Catalyst

It is important that we surround ourselves with people with whom we can be open and honest. We all go through difficult times. You are not alone. Self-care is important and knowing what you need in difficult times is not always easy. Having someone there to listen and support is so important. It is ok to not always be ok. Everyone handles challenges differently. The stress we carry whether from work or home can drain us. Sometimes we are so deep into our unhappiness that we don't realize how it is impacting ourselves and those around us.

Maki Moussavi is a mindset and executive coach who wrote the book *The High Achiever's Guide*. It's about feeling stuck, wanting change, and being terrified of how to make it happen. Her book helps people navigate transition, identify their conditioning and uplevel their mindset. This includes how to deal with toxic behaviors, how false positivity can be limiting, and many more tips/tools for driven, high achieving people. Many times, we have barriers in our way that we need to acknowledge and work on before we can take our career to the next level.

Reflection

- How do you see stress and being overwhelmed affecting your health and well-being?
- What is in your self-care toolbox?
- Who can you turn to when times get tough?

Chapter 13

The First Few Meetings

On Monday morning, Allison texted Mike to say that she'd had some cancellations and was free to chat if he wanted to move their meeting to that day.

He quickly responded. "Absolutely. My schedule is free. What else do I have to do?" He was trying to be funny but also it was true.

When they met at the coffee shop, Allison noticed a change in him. It was a lightness she did not see the first time they met. "You seem to be feeling better."

Mike loved that people could see the change in him. "I am. It is odd how a switch can flip when you know you're not alone. I just didn't know how unhappy I was. Is that odd to say?"

Allison knew what he meant. "Yes, we get so caught up in the churn and trying to be everything to everyone that we don't realize how soul-sucking it can be."

"I needed this break to realize how lost I was," he shares. "And I can't wait to hear more about John."

Allison smiles and jumps right in. "The first meeting with John was a lot like our first meeting but I was sitting in your chair sharing my story. I was telling him how hard I was working and how I was so good at my job. Then John dropped the bomb on me."

Now Mike was really excited. *What was the bomb?*

Allison continues, "He asked me what new skills I was learning through all these promotions. Was I growing as a leader or was I just moving up the organizational chart?"

Both Mike and Allison wince. That was a tough question. Reflecting back, Allison remembered the way she felt when John asked her that question. "I went numb. I was just moving up and sawing people down in my wake. I was successful in my work but not with people."

"Wow, that had to be hard. What did John do next?" Mike asks.

"He told me we would work through it but I had to commit to making changes," Allison shares. "He explained that he had a program that he created early in his career to help people gain the leadership skills they need to keep moving up to the next level. These skills were important no matter anyone's stage or level in their career."

Mike was now taking notes.

"John's program had six topics. He said if I was willing to do it, he would be by my side through the ups and downs. And he was."

The first assignment that John gave her was to understand what type of leader she was, and who she wanted to be. She spent a very thoughtful month having conversations with people around her about how they perceived her. She did a lot of listening, doing several assessments, and digging into the mistakes that she made in her career. She had to figure out how she would have done it differently if she had it to do over. It was a painful step, but she knew that it was going to get her to where she wanted to be, and she had to stick with it.

One conversation with a former peer really hit her hard. Allison had asked, "When you think about me at work, what words come to mind?"

The response came: "hard-driving, no-nonsense, and ruthless."

That really hurt, and I thought, *"Ouch, why did I ask her? I don't think she ever liked me."*

Allison was going to blow it off, but she heard John's voice in her head that this was not going to be easy, so she reached out and asked for a quick phone call. To her surprise, the former coworker agreed.

The call was short and honest, and it forced Allison to face some realities. "People knew they could depend on you to get things done, but they weren't always sure you would have their back. We didn't want to be on a project with you because we weren't confident that you would share the credit. At times you can be a real asshole."

"Whew, that was hard to digest," Allison confesses.

When Allison met with John again to convey what she discovered, he assured her that it would not get easier. "In order to grow, we have to do the work," he says. "Lean into what you learned to uncover even more."

The next step was to understand how she engaged with other people. She was a talker, and quite frankly, any time a question was in the room, she had an answer. One area of growth was discovering how to have thoughtful conversations. John challenged her to listen more and talk less.

Allison did not realize that her behavior was silencing the introverts in the room. She also didn't realize that she often dismissed other people's input because she thought she had all the right ideas. She knew that, more often than not, her gut was right. However, just because she was right didn't mean that she had the right to cut people off. She was not having thoughtful conversations with people.

Additionally, she didn't know how to view other people's perspectives since she was raised in a rather homogeneous community. Allison had to create an awareness of her unconscious bias, which resulted in blind spots in accepting everyone's differences. She was not open to other people's points of view, and that could create an environment where people didn't feel like they belonged. It was unintentional, but because she had not been exposed to people from different backgrounds; she didn't know how to comprehend other people's views.

Her high school had people who appeared on the surface to be diverse, but the cultural norms and views were very similar. She went to a large university and was very active on campus. It wasn't until this reflection exercise that she realized was just surrounding herself with people who looked like her and who all came from similar backgrounds. She had "diverse" friends but she didn't understand what other people were going through and didn't take the time to ask the questions that would lead to her understanding. She didn't even know she had blind spots!

She also had to appreciate that when people said they loved how honest she was, they didn't always mean it. What they meant was they knew where they stood with her but what they didn't like was how she dished out the truth. She had to learn how to have difficult conversations and come from a very caring place without taking people down in the process. Building those relationships was so important for her because then she could separate the action from the person.

During this process, Allison learned a lot about emotional intelligence and how her behavior didn't just impact her, but those around her—what she said and what she didn't say had an effect on others. She now has that knowledge to get to the next step.

When Allison finished describing the first three sessions, she could see Mike was taking it all in. He says, "Wow, that is a lot of work."

She smiles. "Yes, it was, and it was not easy. Thank goodness John kept pushing me."

She glanced down at her watch. "Oh shoot. I have to run. Can you meet next Monday? I will go over the final three topics with you."

Mike was disappointed, but he knew she was busy. "Of course. I'll see you next week!"

Be the Catalyst

As we grow as leaders, there are many skills for us to improve. When we look at who we are as a leader, we focus on integrity, authenticity, humility, responsibility, dependability, and commitment.

Once we know who we are, we look at how we engage with others. This includes communicating with clarity, respect, kindness, active listening, cooperation, coordination, and verbal/non-verbal engagement.

Creating an environment of acceptance is also vital. Understanding our unconscious biases, building trust and psychological safety, raising awareness, being diversity brave as well as creating a culture of inclusion. We want people to feel like they belong and not just that they have to fit in.

Unconscious bias as defined by unconsciousbiasproject.org is defined as prejudice in favor of or against one thing, person, or group compared with another, usually in a way considered to be unfair. Unconscious bias can manifest in many ways, such as how we judge and evaluate others, or how we act toward members of different groups.

Reflection

- What unconscious biases do you have?
- How can you act with more integrity, authenticity, humility, responsibility, dependability, and commitment?
- How are you creating an environment of acceptance? And if you're not, what changes could you make to create psychological safety in your organization?

Chapter 14

Allison's New Path

The rest of that week was pretty uneventful. Mike resumed his regular routines——getting up early, heading to the gym, and then setting up networking meetings or attending events. He knew he had to get back to business. He only had four months of severance, so he needed to get some plans in place if the job in Allison's company didn't work out.

When the next Monday morning came around, he could not wait to see Allison. He had such a busy week, and he wanted to share his developments. She showed up a few minutes late, and he could tell she was frazzled. "I am so sorry. I had an employee who needed to chat with me. I could tell it was important, so I wanted to give him my full attention."

Mike still had no place to be, so he wasn't in a hurry. "No worries. I have plenty of time."

She appreciated his grace. "Being on time is so important to me. I want everyone to know I value their time and respect them," she shares. "I follow the philosophy that if you're early, you're on time; if you're on time, you're late; and if you're late, it is unacceptable."

Mike had never heard that before. "Wow, that is intense!"

Allison knew not everyone understood it. "I just don't want anyone to feel that I think my time is more important than theirs. If they are stuck waiting on me when they can do something else, they might feel I don't appreciate them."

Mike got it. "I never saw it that way, but it makes sense." He loved that nugget. *Keep the lessons coming.*

"Are you ready to jump back in?" Allison asks.

Mike nodded, and she picked up where she left off.

During the fourth month that John was working with Allison, he emphasized the importance of building strong teams. Allison burdened herself by not delegating tasks because she could do them herself. She didn't want to seem weak by asking questions or "pawning off" her work. She could get it done, and she didn't need anyone else's help. Allison had no clue about the importance of teamwork in an organization, and she had created unintentional silos when people didn't want to work with her. She didn't know how much she didn't know about the organization because she was working just on her own projects. She did not comprehend that a strong team could make you more successful. When a leader surrounds themselves with people that complement their work, they're more effective. No one can be good at everything. Understanding what you can and cannot do makes the job easier, but she had to learn this.

"Did that make you feel weak or nervous that people will exploit your gaps?" Mike asks.

This was a feeling that that old Allison had quite a bit. She did not want people to think she was not capable. "Of course. I grew up grinding it out. You figure it out and get it done. Once I really understood that I did not have to do it alone, I became more productive, and my relationships became much stronger."

Mike nodded and she moved on.

In the fifth month, she was hot. *How much longer are we going to do this?* She never said anything to John because she knew that he was successful. She knew that there had to be some secret that he was going to reveal at the end. Her assignment was to pay attention to how she got things done and what goals she had for herself.

"You work each day on tasks, but what are your ultimate goals?" John inquires.

The answer was that while she knew what she wanted to be and where she wanted to go, she didn't have an exact plan on how she was going to do it. She also was not a list maker; getting projects across the finish line was not her strong suit. She had big ideas and was always excited about them, but they typically fizzled out in the final stages. She didn't understand why, but she knew that she had to get to the bottom of it. She started journaling and setting goals. She began a morning routine where she would get up early to exercise, journal, read, and meditate.

The final time she met with John, he spent all of the time talking about the mistakes and the missteps she has made. Some of his questions were:

- How did she react to those mistakes and what did she do?
- What would she have done better?

Allison was now getting frustrated with John. "Didn't we cover this already? Why do we keep talking about this?" she asks.

John laughs. This was his favorite part of coaching people. This was where we reflect on how we reacted. These are the parts where we realize we had it in us all along. We didn't pivot when we needed to. We didn't lean in and have perseverance. We didn't muster up enough grit to push through the barriers. This was the so-what of it all. "When we understand our missteps, we can work hard not to repeat the history that we make," he explains.

John then gave Allison her assignment for the next two weeks. He invited her to reflect on how she could delegate some of her responsibilities, how best to communicate her needs, and where she wanted to be in one-year and five years. She was also to work on how she builds strong relationships with others on the team to get work done, and how resilient she was when things did not go right.

The frustration was really growing now. *We did all this work for what? Is he going to tell me what we are doing with all this? I thought we were done. Why more questions?*

Alison's last comment before they left that coffee was, "So what? What are we doing next?"

And John says, "That's what we'll talk about in two weeks."

Be the Catalyst

Leadership is a journey. It takes time for us to walk through the different levels of who we want to be as a leader. It is ok to be frustrated or to feel like you are not making progress at the speed at which you would like. Believing in the process and getting a strong coach or advisor to hold you accountable will help you get over the times when you feel like you want to give up.

Often in our life, we have shown persistence and grit. However, we don't talk about it often, so we forget how strong and powerful we can be when times are hard. It is important for us to not just celebrate our successes, but to realize we often overcome very challenging times.

Reflection

- How do you practice resilience and grit when things get challenging?
- What actions are you taking that are creating your own challenges?
- What is your vision for the next year?

Chapter 15

The So What

Mike enjoyed learning from Allison. But at times, he was so surprised by her persistence through this process. "Oh, my goodness. What did you do?"

"What could I do?" she comments. "I had come that far. I had to figure out what the purpose of the program was. I didn't come this far to quit."

He could not wait to hear the end, so Mike did not ask another question. She continued to share her journey.

A couple of weeks later Allison and John met to follow up on the work that she had done for the first six months. This was the so-what of it all.

"Did you reflect on the work you have done?" John asks.

"Yes, I realized that to be a strong leader I need to be open, accepting, have deeper conversations and not be afraid to ask for help," Allison shares.

John smiles and nods. "Yes, leadership is a journey. It is not something that you get to a point and stop. You have to keep growing, reflecting, and doing the work."

She now knew she needed to intentionally work on her leadership skills. It was imperative to grow her network and surround herself with strong leaders she could learn from. It was vital to be able to recognize when there wasn't strong leadership and most importantly, to be more self-aware.

This was not easy for an overachiever who prided herself on being a perfectionist, but more importantly, prides herself on awards and recognition for the hard-driving work that she had done. The reflection that she had over the work with John resulted in her seeing that the first stage and level of her career was more about the people she surrounded herself with. Her career level now was about adding inspiration and supporting the team, growing those around her, and removing barriers.

"How would you work through this process?" Allison asks Mike.

"I would have quit halfway through," he quips.

Allison reassured him that there were many times that she thought the coaching with John was wasting her time, but she knew John and she knew his reputation. She trusted him and was intrigued to figure out what the secret was at the end. In the work that Allison continues to this day, she constantly thinks back to the advice, support, and frank conversations that she had with John.

Then she shared the kicker––the connection that Mike had not made. Allison was now a highly successful vice president at John's company.

"John continues to be an advisor to me, and he still supports me to grow in my career. He is a kind advisor willing to tell me when I am acting like an asshole," she adds.

Mike was blown away. "I thought the story would end well. Look at where you are. I never realized John was your CEO."

Allison nods. "Yes, he saw the work I had done and offered me a low-level position that I was probably overqualified for. I accepted it immediately."

All Mike could say was "WOW." *This was a great story, but how can I take it and get myself to my next spot?*

Allison then says, "I can't offer you much, but I would love to have you join the team. You will have the opportunity to grow, and I will continue to coach you."

"I appreciate the offer," he admits. "I'll have to think about it. I know I need to do the work. I want to make sure that I'm ready to get it done."

Mike spent the next few days again reflecting on the opportunity and talking to his parents at the next family dinner. "So, I got a job offer. It is a step back, but I think it has potential."

His dad had an inquisitive look on his face. "That sounds promising. What will you be selling now?"

"Nothing. It is not in sales. It is in product development," Mike says proudly. "I know it's not what I've done in the past, but I really think I need a change."

After he finished speaking, he made eye contact with his mom. He could see the happiness in her expression. "Mike, that's great! Is this with the woman you had coffee with?"

He nods. "Yes, she is a great leader and really believes I have a chance to become a strong leader. It is a pay cut, but I can pay my bills. I also might just be happier."

He could not tell how his dad was feeling. *Is he happy for me or concerned about the step back?* His dad stood up and walked over to give him a hug. "This can't be easy. I am glad you are doing the work. Times have really changed from when I was in business. You have to do what's right for you."

Mike had never felt this connected to his dad. This was the first time he really felt his dad was proud of him.

As had become his normal routine, after dinner with his parents, he met his friends at the pub for football. When he arrived, everyone was there but Julie. He was disappointed because he wanted to share his big news with her. He was going to be her coworker. She had changed his life. He sent her a text. "Are you coming tonight?"

She did not respond for a couple of hours. "I'm sorry I missed seeing you. I had a date, and it went longer than I thought."

Mike was excited for Julie. She had shared with him that she was ready to settle down and get married. In the past, he had quipped that he still had a lot of life to live before being tied down.

Her response was always, "Wait till you meet that one. Your life will change and thaw your cold heart." Every time she said it, she thought, *I can't wait for that day—when Mike meets the woman who knocks him off his feet.*

The following Monday morning, Mike sent Allison a text. "Do you have time for a quick phone call?"

She responded quickly. "Better yet, I am at the coffee shop. Do you want to meet me? I have time."

Ten minutes later, he walked in the door and was surprised to see Julie sitting with Allison. Julie stood up and said, "I was just leaving, but I heard you were coming and wanted to say 'hi.'"

"Stay if you can," he suggests.

She looks at Allison, and Allison nods, so Julie sat back down.

After some pleasantries, Mike told them, "I am excited to join the team. I know that it is a step back in my career, but it is too good to pass up."

Allison is thrilled. "Well, thank goodness. We are lucky to have you!"

Julie became overwhelmed with emotion. She was so proud of the work he had done in such a short time. She could not wait to be his teammate and continue to watch him grow. And she was always inspired by the work that Allison so graciously shared to help people grow in their careers.

Be the Catalyst

As leaders, when we take time to invest in our people, they will return the investment more often than not. When we hire the right people and help them grow, we set them up for success, and this makes our jobs easier. This goes back to self-determination theory and my Catalyst Workplace Model. When we hire people and create a community for them, train them to do the job, and give them the autonomy to do their job, research shows they are happier, more loyal, and more efficient at work.

Research also proves that a well-planned employee training program positively impacts engagement for 93% of employees. Employees also report that due to a lack of development opportunities, they are not able to reach their full potential.

Sometimes we put people in a position where it is not a good fit for one reason or another. Don't let this discourage you. Keep leaning into your people and find ways to develop them.

Reflection

- How are you giving your people the development they need and crave?
- How might you improve your development program?
- How might you improve in hiring the right people?

Chapter 16

A Brand-New Day

Sunday dinner with the family turned into a great celebration for Mike's first day of work. When he walked into his parent's house, everyone was already there. *What's going on? They are always late.* He thought about his sisters.

"Surprise!" Everyone cheered when he walked in. His mom handed him a glass of champagne.

She was so excited for him. "Tonight, it is all about you. We can't wait to see where this next road takes you!"

"I don't know what to say." Mike was stunned. It had been a long time since he had given his family something to celebrate. These last few months, and really years, had been a struggle. He did not realize how unhappy he was and how miserable he must have been to be around.

"New job and maybe new girl?" His youngest sister winked at him.

Mike winces. "Let's slow down. One thing at a time. I am still figuring out my new job. I have to keep working on myself before I can bring someone else into this."

His mom and sisters feigned disappointment. Then they all started to laugh. They had such an amazing dinner. First time in a long time, he could really enjoy himself and not feel secret resentment to all the success his sisters were having.

On Mike's first day, he woke up early, so excited to start his new journey——and a little overwhelmed at the same time. *What am I doing? Can I do this?*

Allison had sent him an agenda of activities that he expected to accomplish and/or attend not just on his first day but for his first thirty days with the organization. She had laid out when and whom he would meet with, whom he was going to have lunch with on the first day, and recommendations on people he should contact. She wanted to ensure on day one that he felt like he was a part of the team.

She even provided details about their culture and what to expect on Fridays; it was more of a casual day where everyone wore jeans, whereas the rest of the week, they did business casual. She wanted to make sure he was not overdressed or underdressed. She shared that on the third Wednesday of every month, they ordered breakfast as an organization so he shouldn't eat breakfast that day and join in the fun. All of the little details that were important to the culture were laid out for him.

When his first day arrived, he walked into the building. Before he opened the door, he paused to take a deep breath. The doubts resurfaced. *Am I ready for this? Will I be successful? What am I doing? Be open. Don't be an asshole.*

"Mike, welcome to our company!" He was greeted excitedly by a young man working the front desk. As he glanced around, Mike saw his name on the board behind the front desk. "We've been eager to meet you!"

Wow, this had never happened before. In previous jobs, he showed up and felt like they did not even know he was starting work. It seemed as if they were not prepared for him at all. Immediately, he could tell this company was very different.

The young man led Mike to his new cubicle, and on the desk was a welcome basket with all kinds of organizational goodies and trinkets. There was also a small plant sitting in one corner––and a handwritten note from John welcoming him to the organization.

"Mike, We are thrilled to have you join our team. We have heard so much about you and can't wait to have you contribute to the team! We are also looking forward to getting to know you and learning from you. If you need anything, I am always open to hearing how we can do things better!"

Before Mike could even dig into his basket, Allison was at his desk, handing him a coffee mug with the organization and his name on it––and full of coffee.

"I am so excited that you are here! How are you doing?"

"Great, and a little nervous. Maybe a bit overwhelmed."

"You're in good hands. We will all take care of you. IT has set up your desk but if you need anything, let me know!"

He laughed. "I don't know about this crazy-looking keyboard." She reassured him that she loved her ergonomic keyboard, but it wasn't for everyone, so if it didn't fit him, she would get him whatever keyboard he needed.

When she walked off, he sat there in silence. This was definitely different than anything he has experienced. In his first job, he spent the whole day with Joe but did not get to meet anyone else. He did not know where he fit in yet, but within the first few hours, he had no doubt that they wanted him there.

Throughout the morning, his new peers stopped by his desk to introduce themselves. They made sure he knew how they might interact, their role in the organization, and what type of work gave them energy, so if he ever needed help in those areas, he would know where to turn.

Julie popped by before he headed to HR to do his paperwork. "How is everything going?"

Mike could not believe that so far, it was all she said it was. "So far, so good. But it is just the first day. It is a bit crazy. Everyone is so nice."

Julie was not surprised by his answer. "It helps when you're happy at work. We all get along. Sounds cliché, but it is true!"

Mike was hopeful that he would continue this feeling as well. "Do you all ever have a bad day?"

"Oh, heck, yes! We just let each other know. Sometimes you wake up, and you're just not feeling it. We are all human!" Julie shares.

Mike smiles. He thought, *First crack in the façade. Here we go!* "Now, here we go. It is not perfect!"

"Of course not. Nothing is perfect. We just communicate with each other. When someone is having a bad day, they will let people know upfront. That way, when we are not our normal selves or maybe snap at someone, we know there is something going on." Julie continues, "Or if we notice someone is a little off, we will pull them aside and check on them."

Mike wondered what the catch was.

"You'll find your groove," Julie assures him. "Come on. I will walk you to HR."

Be the Catalyst

How we set our people up for success has many important steps. I firmly believe that how we start people with our organization is the foundation of the working relationship. This is when we begin to integrate them into the team and create a sense of belonging for the new employee. This is when we start to create a community for them.

Everyone has different levels of expectations for work relationships. There are many benefits to strong working relationships. When we feel connected to our work, there is increased satisfaction with our career as well as increased comfort with sharing our thoughts/opinions with our teams. Higher levels of relationships also improve productivity for all team members because of enhanced communication. This also allows for moral support and assistance with meeting challenging timelines as well as tasks. All of this can lead to higher retention rates.

Reflection

- What expectations do you have of your work relationships?
- How are you creating stronger relationships at work?
- Where might you need to improve your relationship-building skills?

Chapter 17

The Team Lunch

When he finished with human resources, Mike walked back to his area where Allison and the team were waiting to go to lunch. They had a favorite spot around the corner, and they wanted to include Mike. "We eat here quite often," she says, as they entered the restaurant. "You're always welcome to join us. The food is great, and the service is even better."

"This place is great," Mike says. "Julie and I come here quite a bit for happy hour and to watch football."

"Then you will be right at home with the team," Allison responds.

The owner approached, extending his hand to Mike. "Mike, I heard the rumor. Julie told me you were joining the team. I am excited for you."

When Mike sat down at the table, the uneasiness kicked in again. There were a few people on the team he wasn't sure how he would get along with because they were significantly younger and earlier in their careers. *What possibly could we have in common?* There were a few seasoned professionals that were closer to his age. They were a step above him on the organizational charts. Imposter syndrome began setting in. *Is this going to work? Do I belong here? What if this is a mistake?*

As lunch continued, he was pleasantly surprised as they laughed, joked, and shared stories about their families and their careers and about their friends and what they enjoyed doing outside of work. Mike was, at times, a very private person and wasn't used to divulging personal information at work, but he loosened up a little. The older gentleman across the table asks, "Tell us about yourself. Married, girlfriend?"

This made him so uncomfortable. *Well, now is as good a time as ever to jump right into this.* "Nope, single, and never married," he shares. "However, I am becoming more open to finding someone. I have just been so busy with my career that I haven't had a lot of time. And I have work to do on myself before taking this next step."

Julie chimes in, "Well, now I am on a mission."

"Slow down," he warns. "It is bad enough I have to deal with this between my mom and sisters. I don't need to hear it at work."

One of the women at the end of the table says, "Well, we will do it on the down low."

The guy sitting next to Mike laughs. "Hold on. Now, you have done it. They all have a mission."

Oh no, what have I done? Mike quickly changed the subject. The team understood that what they had built could be a little intimidating to come right into. They had been together for quite a while, so they were used to being very open and teasing each other. The last new hire was about seven months ago, so they knew how this went. It could be a culture shock for some people if they didn't understand how the team worked.

Sara, the newest team member, leans over and says, "This group can be overwhelming at first but you settle in quickly."

Another team member got the attention of the table. "Mike, we are thrilled to have you here. We hope you feel welcome and that you can jump right in with us."

Another member teases, "We may seem scary because we have been together so long, but we really are not."

Julie smiles as the team was all welcoming Mike. She knew he had never experienced anything like this. She leans over to

Allison. "Thank you!" Allison nods. She knew that this meant so much to Julie that Allison was willing to bring Mike on the team and give him a chance.

Allison had not shared Mike's history with the team, so he was coming in with a clean slate, but Mike was still very worried about what they knew and had heard about him. He was confident he could do the job, but he wasn't convinced that he could build the relationships and have the humility that Allison conveyed was so important.

When they got back to the office, Mike needed a few minutes to take this all in. He would not consider himself an introvert, but this had all been a bit overwhelming. It had just been five hours since he walked in the front door of the company, but he was exhausted. He had a lot of new information to digest. Plus, he wasn't used to going this deep with people this quickly, even if some people would think he had not shared much.

In the past, he would come to work and start grinding, and then he would leave. Yet, he liked the different culture. *I think I can get used to this!*

Be the Catalyst

Building a strong team takes work. It is about building relationships and understanding how we work and who we are individually and collectively. This does not require grand gestures. It does need time to get to know each other. Whether we make intentional time during meetings or have a team lunch, it gives everyone time to connect. In full transparency, I know not everyone loves these activities. It is ok. As we get to know what our people like and need, we can find ways to make that work for our teams.

Relationships are what help us remove people from tasks. I have found that in my career as I build stronger relationships with people, I can have more difficult conversations with them. They realize that I care about them but sometimes they make a mistake that needs to be corrected.

Reflection

- What are some of the ways that you are doing intentional work to connect your people to each other?
- What's your comfort level with difficult conversations?
- How are you helping your people reach their full potential?

Chapter 18

Laying Out the Expectations

The next day, Mike was feeling even more energized. His first day finished off strong, and his confidence was building as it went on. He was really learning what was expected of him and how he was expected to get it done. He showed up early so he could get settled before he started his day of meetings.

First up, Mike and Allison met in her office to check in on his first day and to jump into his onboarding. When she had previously explained the onboarding process, she told him, "We don't expect you to know everything in the first day, week, or even year. You will be learning things as you go. Don't feel like you need to be an expert."

After some quick pleasantries, she pulled out the company training development guide. She explained to him that everyone, at all levels, had the same initial onboarding. "We want everyone to be on the same page!"

She walked him through the workplace model that they lived every second of every day. "This is more than a poster! This model is about creating an environment where people feel like they belonged and were connected," she explains.

The importance of acceptance and creating safety in the organization was very evident. No matter what level an employee was at, they were encouraged to speak up and speak out. As long as it was respectful and about the projects or behavior, and not about the people, everyone was always welcome to engage.

She reviewed the importance of having the tools and the training/development to do the job. "While we don't have a large budget, we want to make sure that you have what you need to perform the core functions of your job. If there are any tools or supplies that you need, please let us know."

Then she revealed his personal development plan, something that was put in place for all new employees. This plan laid out the training he would participate in over the next six months and the milestones he could expect as he completed it. It also outlined the different senior leaders he would meet with over the next few months. She described their teams to ensure he understood how his role played a pivotal part in the whole organization. "We all are important to the success of the organization," she emphasizes. "No team or person is more critical than the other. Without all of us pushing in the same direction, we can't reach our full potential."

Mike got it but could not resist defending his previous role. "Yes, but without sales, you don't have money coming in. Right?"

Allison knew this would be the first of many important lessons for Mike. "They are important. Think about it though. Without a great product, they would have nothing to sell. If it is not packaged correctly with the correct instructions, it might not be useful to our customers. And after the sales teams make the sale, if we don't offer great service, customers won't come back. Then if we don't bill correctly, that can be frustrating. I won't even go into all the other backend functions. I will leave that to the different vice presidents," she adds.

This was the first time someone really laid it out like that to Mike. "Well, that makes a lot of sense. I never saw it like that."

Mike was beginning to understand the organization's expectations and realize that it wanted to make sure that all employees had the same level of common sense and knew what was expected of them––how to do the job and what the job looked like as well as their crucial role in the organization. Alison also wanted to ensure that he understood his job, the tasks, and that the team that was proud of what they do.

The next conversation was one that Mike had never had before. The conversation was about Allison's leadership philosophy.

"Mike, I share this with everyone on my team and everyone I work with. It is important for you to understand who I am as a leader. I believe my job is to help you grow and to help you have the best opportunity to succeed," she explains.

She described the different assessments that she had taken, and feedback that she had received as a vice president of the organization, not just from her boss, or her peers, but also from others in her organization, those that worked with her and for her.

"I discovered some gap areas where I'm not as confident, and I have more work to do," she admits. "And I hope you'll help me grow in these areas as well. I'm still a work in progress."

"What do you need to work on?" Mike asks with surprise. In his mind, she looked like she had it all together.

"I am continuing to help my team grow. I have problems delegating sometimes because I want to make sure I set my team up for success. I don't want to burden them with my projects. I know this is not the right thought, so I have to keep reminding myself. As an extrovert, I also need to remind myself to take deep breaths and not let my excitement dominate a conversation. I give you permission to hold me accountable for the things I am working on," she offers.

"So how do you want to be managed, Mike?" she asks. "How do you learn best?"

Mike was surprised by this whole conversation. This was all a bit overwhelming. *First, she admits that she is not perfect and now she is asking me to tell her how to manage me.* He had never been asked this type of question. "I am not really sure. I know that I have a lot to learn and want to get better. I also know that I have bad habits I need to break. I want my leadership to be authentic, honest, and to trust me to do my job!"

"What are those bad habits? Can you name them?" Allison asks.

"I need to be open to hearing other people's feedback and to focus on building relationships with the team. I am used to working alone so this will be very different for me," he explains. "And there's probably more I haven't identified."

"We will go there!" she chuckles.

Finally, she sketches out how they get work done. "There are core functions in everyone's jobs that they have to do whether they liked it or not. Plus, I do like to give you an opportunity to stretch and to help you grow. For the next several months, you'll be really busy just learning the job, but I want to be able to nurture your other areas of interest," she explains. "I could pull you in on projects or meetings."

"Do you do this for the whole team?" Mike asks. "You have fifteen people reporting to you. How do you have time for all of this and get your job done?"

"My job is my people," Allison quickly answers. "As a leader in the organization, who is on the executive team, it is not just about my direct reports, but about the whole organization. I am always asking: How could the executive team provide more leadership and support?"

Be the Catalyst

No workplace is perfect. There is always work to do to help have a safe and healthy culture. Setting expectations for the team is important as well as having a strong vision. Your people want to know what is expected of them and how they will be held accountable. It is in vagueness we set our people up to fail.

Organizations too often expect people to come in with common sense. The challenge with common sense is that it is not common until we discuss it and lay it out. How can we hold people accountable if we never share expectations with them? Not only should we share the expectations, but leaders need to be bought in and model the behavior. It is important for our people to see us living the values that we say we believe in.

Leaders must also be reminding and weaving the values into the work that they do. The values should be top of mind for everyone. Too often organizations will create a mission and value statement, a strategic plan, or other documents but never revisit them. This should be a regular practice to make sure you are aligned with whom you say you are.

Reflections

- How are you setting clear expectations for your team?
- How are you sharing your vision?
- How are you ensuring your vision and goals are aligned?

Chapter 19

Settling In and the Six-month Review

During the first couple of days, Mike had to admit he wasn't sure he was going to make it on the team. He was having some serious imposter syndrome issues. *Do I really belong here? Can I do this job? Everyone is so nice. Will they think I am an asshole?* He had to remind himself that everyone felt this way at times but he could do it with the support of the company and the team.

He slowly settled in, and Allison never gave up on him. As he began his second week in the organization, John popped over to his cubicle just to check in.

"Hi, Mike, how is everything going?'

Mike looked up in surprise to see it was John. *How does he have time to worry about me?* "Great, I am still learning a lot."

"With anything new, there's always an adjustment," John assures him. "Do you need anything? I know I've said this before, but it is really important to me that everyone feels that they belong and that you have the tools and resources you need to do your job!" John frequently reinforced the importance of autonomy in the workplace. "We want you to feel trusted to do your job!"

Over the next several months, Mike found that the organization didn't just have words on a poster that was ignored. The leaders and team members lived the values of the company. They regularly had activities and tools where people could give feedback on their sense of belonging. They had opportunities for the teams to get together to learn from each other and meet with people from all different backgrounds and experiences.

The company also invested in its people. In his short time, not only did Mike have his onboarding plan but had begun to work on his career plan. Over the months, as Mike met with the different leaders, they asked him about his aspirations and what experiences he would like to have. They all encouraged him to reach out at any time if he was curious about the work they or their team was doing.

The organization valued feedback and growth, so every month, employees met with their leaders to track their progress. The six-month check-in was a big one. This was to ensure that everyone was on the same page and was living the company's values. It was a time to discuss any challenges or concerns with the job fit. They had this conversation with all new employees.

Mike had been with the organization for six months, and some days felt like he was doing a great job and other days were just reminders of how much work on his leadership skills remained undone. He'd never been on a team that was so open to giving critical feedback. He was used to doing projects, making sales, and handing them off, and then it was someone else's issue. However, this team was engaging and had lively meetings where no one was immune to "feedback."

During his six-month review with Allison, he experienced more firsts in the workplace. Allison led off by asking, "Did you bring your peer feedback with you?"

Mike sheepishly pulled out a sheet of paper of comments, both the good and bad that others in the organization and on his team had given him. Some of the comments were that he should speak up more, and others were that he needed to be open to feedback. He was told that people didn't know him and that they wanted to get to know who he was. "These were pretty hard for me to hear because I am not used to this type of workplace," he explains. "I know I still have things to work on. For instance, I know I must keep working on my relationship building outside of our department. When I get busy or stressed, I fall back into the blame game. Luckily for me, the culture is so healthy that my teammates will help me realize what I am doing."

"I know this is different, and it is not always easy. That is why humility is so important to us," Allison says. "I talked to John about your first six months and mentioned that I was worried that you have been falling back into some of your old behaviors when you are stressed or busy. I am so happy you recognized it and mentioned it before I did."

Again, Mike felt uneasy and like he was being punched in the gut. *Here we go. I am going to be fired!*

Allison could quickly tell this was hard for Mike to hear so she continued. "However, John and I agree that it is important for you to go through the Emerging Leaders' Program."

"Really? I'm so much older than the other people in the program," he says a bit surprised. "How am I a fit?"

"This is less about age and more about where you are in your career journey. We want to make sure that you have the critical skills that I grew over my time working with John as an advisor," she assures. "The next cohort begins in a month. I want you to think about the next steps in your career."

Mike thought this was very interesting because he had only been there six months. *How was she already thinking about the next steps?* He reassured her that he would think about it.

During the next one-on-one, Mike accepted the nomination for the Emerging Leaders' Program. *What do I have to lose?* At this point in his career, he had been to what he thought was the top of the mountain and then shoved off of it. Then he realized that he was shoved off from his own doing. It was time for him to buckle down and figure out how he was going to live the last half of his career journey.

Allison was thrilled, and she assured him that he was not alone in the process. "I'll be here supporting you as well as the rest of the executive team. We'll make sure that the program fits your needs."

As their conversation continued, Mike learned that he would be getting an advisor in the program—not necessarily someone to mentor him on the skills that he needed to do his job but more about soft skills.

He'd be asked to reflect upon a few questions as well, such as: How does he build relationships? How does he communicate? How does he get things done? How he builds strong teams?

And his advisor would hold him accountable for doing his work.

Be the Catalyst

It is important to talk about imposter syndrome here. Imposter syndrome is the feeling you're a fraud or that you don't have the skills to do the job. It is also the feeling that other people realize you can't do the job. First, we must acknowledge this is a real thing and most people experience it at some point in their careers. Also, understand you're not alone. There are ways to get around these feelings. Make a list of your accomplishments and review it often. Recognize the hard work you have done. Finally, don't expect yourself to be perfect. No one is perfect and it is unfair to yourself to set that expectation.

There are many ways to break through imposter syndrome, but it does take very intentional work. We need to be honest with ourselves and acknowledge that we are feeling it. The next step is to recognize you're being hard on yourself and find ways to celebrate your successes.

Reflection

- How might imposter syndrome lurk in your and your team's consciousness? What can you do to acknowledge it and tame it?
- Who is in your network that can be your cheerleader and support you when you are feeling imposter syndrome?
- What would you tell a friend who is experiencing imposter syndrome?

Chapter 20

The Emerging Leaders Program

On the first day of the Emerging Leaders Program, Mike entered the room with a little bit of hesitation about why he was there. *I am too old for this! Why am I doing this to myself?* Soon, however, he was pleasantly surprised as he looked around the room and saw people of all different ages. It wasn't just the twenty-somethings. He immediately relaxed. *OK, this is not what I thought it was going to be. Let's see where I can go with this.*

The Emerging Leaders Program was six months long. The group met for three hours once a month. They dug into the different career and power skills that were vital for leaders at any stage of their career. As skills were being reviewed, Mike was making the connection that these sessions and skills were similar to the story that Allison had shared with him from John's advice.

The first session covered who they were as leaders. They identified the type of leader they currently were and who they want to be as they grew in their leadership. They dove into integrity, authenticity, and humility. The session was led by several members of the executive team, who told stories of times they had to step up and take responsibility to show commitment to their team.

The CFO shares, "It is important to my team to know I have their back. I want them to have the autonomy to do their job in the best way to fit them."

HR chimes in, "Within the guardrails you set. Right?"

The CFO smirks, "Of course. You can't be too creative in accounting. But you can find ways to make your job easier by the flow of work. We also have some old policies that can be updated to make us more efficient."

"What happens then they make a mistake?" HR asks.

"It is so important that we keep that between us. I am not going to put them on blast," explains the CFO. "I will pull them into my office to discuss what happened and how we can make sure it does not happen again. I will then take responsibility for their actions. I am ultimately responsible for my department, so it is on me."

He smiles as he sees those in the class nodding along. "I also make sure I praise in public. When my team does great things, I will share this information with everyone. I will also send them a handwritten note. The team needs to know that I see them and appreciate them."

The group also completed several assessments and had discussions about their successes and growth areas as leaders. They learned about their emotional intelligence (EQ) as well as where they get their energy from work. The discussions were important because the more they learned about themselves, the better they would work with others. Christy, a longtime member of the product team, discussed how uncomfortable she was with the results of her emotional intelligence assessment. "I always thought I was great with people. It hurt when my score was so low."

HR assures, "It is ok. The beauty of EQ is that you can work on it and improve in these areas."

"As soon as I saw the results, I knew that it was when I get passionate or excited, I have to let my tongue catch up with my brain," Christy adds.

"I have been told by many that they can hear my facial expressions," says HR. "I am always working on that. Often, it is unintentional. I don't want to come across like an asshole!"

Christy and several others in the room nodded emphatically in agreement.

Their homework after this session was to create their own leadership philosophy. As they were given the assignment, the executive team shared their philosophies. They discussed how it has evolved throughout their careers. They also admitted some of their biggest missteps in their careers. John went first.

"When I was going through my early career, I just did not know what I did not know. I sometimes had to learn the hard way," John explains.

This story made him uncomfortable, and he paced as he told it. "I was a new manager and thought I could run the company better than my peers. I had been a high achiever my whole life. Not just at work. I rarely failed at anything. It took me many years to realize I was not really having success."

Everyone in the room was leaning forward and hanging on his every word. *What did he do?*

John continues, "There were times I took all the glory rather than share it with my team. I would take credit for group projects. Frankly, I was kind of an asshole. I would stay late so people would know I was working harder than them. I assumed every time a door was closed and people were talking, they were discussing me."

This was hitting Mike hard. *How can our stories be so similar?*

"Then the day that changed my career arrived. My boss called me into her office and told me I was not getting the promotion I thought I would be getting. When I asked why she said that I was not a team player. I can still hear her comments in my head today," he admits. "I often remind myself that everything is not about me. If I don't figure out how not to be so selfish, I will not grow."

Ouch! The room felt the pain for him. Mike asks, "What did you do next?"

"I left her office upset, hurt, and frankly wanted to quit. *She doesn't know what she is talking about.* I later talked to a co-worker I trusted, and they told me the truth about how I acted toward them. They said that at times I really acted like an ass-hole. It really opened my eyes. That day I changed from 'me' to 'us.' That is when my journey took a hard right turn, and I started seeing success in building strong relationships."

"Sounds too good to be true!" Mike remarks.

"Oh no, I had a lot of work to do. I had burned bridges. I had to rebuild trust and let my team and peers know they could depend on me. It was not easy, but it was so worth the work!"

The next session was about communication skills and engagement with others. The group discussed the importance of clarity and respect in the workplace. They played the telephone game to illustrate active listening skills. Mike really enjoyed this session. As a former sales guy, he has always been proud of his communication skills. The group did activities to focus on cooperation and coordination. They analyzed times when the group had projects break down because of a lack of communication.

Their homework during this session was to have a kind conversation. *What is a kind conversation? This is crazy!* The facilitator explains, "Too often, we don't want to hurt people's feelings, so we will just be too nice. We will not tell them the truth because it is hard!" Being nice is the opposite of all leaders' expectations. They were expected to be honest and help people grow!

As the group walked out of class that day, there were lots of discussions on this topic. Cindy says, "I do this all the time. I am always blunt!"

Meredith chimes in. "Yes, but you are not always kind when you do it. Sometimes it hurts!"

Cindy says, "I just don't want people to not know the truth."

Meredith responds, "In the spirit of being kind, I want to share with you that you might not realize how harsh it comes across."

Cindy cringes. "That is never my intention. I just will never say anything behind their back that I won't say to their face. I pride myself on that."

Meredith understood what Cindy is saying so she knew she had to give an example. "Remember when we were in a leadership meeting, and I shared an experience from my previous job?"

Cindy nods and braces herself.

"You shut me down really quick to remind the group that the company was no longer in business. I did not even get a chance to make my point before you shut me down."

Cindy winces. "I just wanted to make sure everyone had context for what you were saying," she explains.

"Yes, true, but you did not know what I was going to say. You could have heard me out before jumping in. It hurt my feelings," Meredith adds.

"Why didn't you say anything to me?" Cindy asks.

"I did not know you well. We have never really talked so I was not sure what I could or could not say!" Meredith responds.

"I am so sorry I acted like such an asshole," Cindy shares. "Definitely part of my emotional intelligence I need to work on."

Be the Catalyst

To create an organization that values growth and development, it is important that all leaders buy in. When our people see leaders investing in themselves and others, they will be more likely to invest in themselves. This also helps individuals in the organization get to know different leaders. This can help build community. It also projects that the leadership team is on the same page and has the same expectations.

This is where we pull back into your leadership philosophy. These guiding principles for yourself and those around you helps with expectations. As you are working with your teams, work to understand their guiding principles and vision. This will help you create a development plan for them.

Reflection

- How are you fostering a culture that values a growth mindset?
- How might you bring more awareness of emotional intelligence into your organization?
- What is your leadership philosophy and how are you living it?

Chapter 21

Keep the Growth Coming

As the group entered the room, there was excitement. Everyone was bantering about the work they had been doing. Mike was telling the group, "Not only did I have several kind conversations, but my teammates took time to have conversations with me as well."

Meredith adds, "The same happened to me. I did have to do some apologizing and explained to many people about my emotional intelligence scores." She pauses and decides to keep going. "I did not realize what an asshole I was being. I just thought I was being honest."

Mike jokes, "Who would have known there is a difference between being nice, kind, or an asshole." He winks.

When the third session was introduced, Mike thought, *Oh, this is going to be a tough one.* This session was on acceptance and they were asked to ponder: How do we be culturally brave and create an environment where everyone feels like they belong and not that they have to be someone they are not to just fit in?

The first topic of the day was psychological safety. The group was all in agreement they had not heard of this term. HR explains, "This is where you believe you will not be punished or humiliated when you speak up, ask questions, or make mistakes. Team members feel they can take risks without shame and will be respected and accepted for who they are."

Cindy jumps in. "I have worked on teams where certain people felt this, but not everyone. Is that psychological safety?" she asks.

"No, it is when everyone feels it," HR adds "Not just some or most of the team members."

"So how do we build it? What do we do?" Cindy questions.

"There are a few basic things that you can do to create psychological safety. First is to model the behavior yourself as a leader. Be open and vulnerable. Share that you trust your team and that you take risks. It is also important to understand their roles and set expectations that are very clear."

The room was listening intently. Many nodded, acknowledging that they remembered a time in their career when they felt like they had to just fit in.

HR led the discussion further on how team building, emotional intelligence, and kind conversations built psychological safety.

The next set of topics often proved tough for many individuals. However, the group was committed to being open and supportive of the conversation around unconscious bias. Mike struggled with this topic. As a white man growing up, he would hear about privilege. He hated the word privilege, so he really had to focus on staying humble during this session.

He worked hard to listen to those in the group. Just because he had not experienced the feelings they were sharing did not mean they were not real. He knew that he was not ever intentionally trying to make people feel they could not be their true selves around him. He had to make an extra effort to hear their story and create an environment where they had opportunities to share their ideas. He quickly learned from the session that no one was blaming him just because he was born into a white middle-class family. His opportunity was to open up seats at the table and provide access to those people who intentionally or unintentionally had their voices silenced.

Even an organization that prided itself so much on belonging still had work to do. Good or bad, people were still falling into what they had known before working for the organization, and that was the challenge for everyone in the room. It can be difficult to escape the often-subtle beliefs and limitations that surround us when we're in our youth. And if we don't take time to question these beliefs, we often carry on harmful and sometimes destructive behaviors. No matter the labels that you display or the labels that you don't talk about, these define who you are. Everyone in the room has a role in making people feel like they belong.

Mike thought the session was going to be a breeze, but he found himself squirming in his own skin. Memories of high school soccer moments floated back reminding him how he wasn't thinking about the team, but himself.

I have been doing this for years. All the way back to when I played soccer in high school.

However, it was likely that Mike had forgotten that he struggled at times to be the best teammate.

HR discussed the importance of building relationships across teams so everyone could be on the same page. "When we work in our individual teams and focus only on our goals, we can create unintentional silos that can harm the greater organization."

This discussion led to deeper conversations about the impact that weak teams can have on organizational success, especially when we don't communicate effectively or when leaders don't look at the full organizational goals when running their teams.

As was becoming more and more normal, when the class was over, no one left the room. The conversations continued on how to use everything they learned. John happened to walk by the room and jumped in.

"This was the class I needed," Meredith shares. "I did not realize how often in my career I did not feel like I was really a part of the team."

"Can you expand on that?" John asks.

"I just keep thinking about a time when I told a man on the executive team at another organization that when I talked, he would either shut me down or explain to the table what I was saying."

"How did that make you feel?" John asks.

"Not only did I feel that I did not have a voice but that when I explained how I was feeling, I felt even more dismissed," Meredith explains. "When I shared my feelings, I was told that he did not feel it was a problem because he did not see it."

The other women in the room nodded in agreement. They had all experienced similar things in their career. Meredith adds, "Some changed their behaviors and others did not care if we thought they were an asshole."

AJ had not said much in the first couple of classes and decided now was the time he could not keep quiet. "As a black man, this happens all too often to me. I am either not invited to meetings or I am invited but don't get opportunities to speak," he shares. "The most discouraging thing for me is when I look around and don't see people who look like me get opportunities to advance."

John nodded and encouraged AJ to continue if he is comfortable sharing more.

"I used to work for a company that talked a lot about their diversity programs, but they did not have any diversity at the decision-making level," he explains. "One of the leaders would say he wanted to hear from everyone, but when we conveyed our thoughts, he would tell us that work needed to be done. Then nothing ever changed. They would never understand that words are just words. Actions are what really tell the story."

Everyone really appreciated AJ's sharing and, more importantly, his willingness to answer their questions as they wanted to understand further how they could support everyone in the organization to create an environment of belonging.

Be the Catalyst

We all come together in the workplace with different experiences and backgrounds. Creating an environment of belonging is about a culture where everyone can show up as their authentic self. When we work to understand who we are and our biases, and acknowledge our potential to have blind spots, it allows us to grow and learn from others. This at times requires challenging our past and stretching who we are as individuals. Building strong relationships and trust allows us to open up to others.

I was challenged to focus on who is in the room and instead of gravitating to people like me, to step out of my comfort zone and join a discussion of people from different backgrounds. This practice has had a powerful change in my relationships and allowed me to expand my thinking.

Reflection

- How are you an inclusive leader?
- How do you support a culture that weeds out unconscious bias?
- How do you facilitate relationships between the organization's teams?

Chapter 22

How Do We Get Stuff Done

After Mike had been in the program for a few months, Allison asks, "How is the Emerging Leaders Program going? Do you love it?"

"You were so right. I appreciate you giving me a chance to go through the program," Mike says. "At first, I was very skeptical. I was not sure at this point in my career what I could learn."

Allison smiled. "Life-long learning. We have to keep growing to keep going."

Mike now understood what she was saying. He appreciated the opportunity to learn more about himself and how he can be a better leader.

Allison continued to find out more about his reaction to the program. "All too often we think we get to a certain point in our career, and we know it all. That is when we really need to lean into our journey. There is always room for growth."

"Yes, I actually gave my dad the emotional intelligence book from our class. This led to interesting dinner conversations recently. My mom really enjoyed hearing about my growth and what I learned."

Later that day, Mike was preparing for session five. This was the session on effectiveness. Their prework for the class was to analyze their productivity, how they schedule their days, and measure their goals.

The group was tasked with setting their goals for the next five years and then breaking them down into one-year goals and weekly tasks. During the class, they were to learn new skills of focusing and organizing their time.

Allison joined the class to talk about obstacles we might put in our way when getting work done. "Often in my career, I thought I needed to do certain things to get ahead. I was always working late or making sure I was seen by those above me."

The class recognized that John had shared a very similar story when he spoke to the class. Mike perked up. *It seems to be a theme that we keep doing things that might not be productive to try to get ahead.*

Allison continues, "I would fill my day with meetings and projects that I might not like or that were not in my area to impress others. I quickly found that when I took on stretch projects, the ones I was passionate about it, it did not matter who knew or saw what I was doing. I was more satisfied with my work. When I was trying to please others, I was more drained and frustrated because I was not getting recognition for my work."

Most in the room could totally relate to this.

"It is important to the leadership team here that everyone works hard but most importantly manages their time well," Allison explains. "We expect you to take time off for yourself and your families. Log off on Friday and don't work after hours. We trust you to get your jobs done."

The final session on resilience was the toughest for Mike. This was a time to reflect on the mistakes he made in his career and how to move forward with a growth mindset. This session focused on agility, self-management, optimism, confidence, open-mindedness, and stress management.

To start the session, they were broken into pairs to reflect on all sessions and the biggest lesson learned. Mike very intentionally partnered with AJ. Mike wanted to make a purposeful connection with him.

"How are you doing, Mike?" AJ asks. "I know you haven't been here for long."

"I thought the acceptance session was going to be hardest. I had no clue the work I needed to do to forgive myself for the mistakes I have made. I also need to view my path as a learning opportunity," Mike shares.

AJ agrees. "This has all been very eye-opening. For me, it was about communication. I learned that I was not giving people kindness or asking for clarity when they said something. I would just get upset and write them off," AJ explains.

Mike appreciated the candor, especially since AJ had been so quiet for most of the classes. "Do you consider yourself an introvert?" he asks.

"No, I am usually quiet until I know that I can trust the room," AJ offers. "You never know what people are thinking. and I don't want to give them excuses to not give me a chance."

Ouch! Mike wondered if he ever made AJ feel like he could not trust him. Mike knew his actions at times could have been harsh.

AJ continues, "Now I know to ask questions and get an understanding of what is being said. If I don't do that, I am not being kind to them."

Mike and AJ both laugh. The idea of being kind and not nice was now a theme for the group. "You can't grow if you don't know!" Mike says.

"We need that on a t-shirt!" AJ high-fives Mike, and they both chuckle.

When the class ended, Mike had mixed feelings. He was happy to have gone through the program but was disappointed it was over. As they left the room, they were reminded by HR that they were far from done. "This is just the beginning. You all have each other and the other leaders in the organization. It is your responsibility to help make us the best we can be!"

At the end of the program––and such a short time with the company, Mike valued his new connections and relationships. There would be days when he would have to push through and remind himself that he is a work in progress. There would be days that he would make mistakes, and he would have to own those and have difficult conversations.

It was important for him to remember in the future there would be days when people would come to him, with crucial conversations to let him know that he messed up, and he had to lean in with humility for the greater good of himself, and the greater good of the organization.

Be the Catalyst

As leaders, understanding how we impact those on our team is very important. If we create the illusion that we are always busy and don't have time for our people, they will not come to us. Knowing our emotional intelligence can help us with this. Paying attention to how we impact those around us and react to the environment is a critical part of emotional intelligence. It also allows us to work on how we pay attention to what is going on around us. Getting ourselves under control and modeling the behavior can settle teams.

We model the behaviors of how those around us work. I also challenge leaders to free up their schedules. There are ways to manage your time effectively so you can make sure you're taking time for yourself and your people. Many times, leaders feel they have to be in *all* meetings. There are times when you can send someone on your team. If you are in meetings and there are multiple people on your team in the room, ask your-self "do we all need to be here?" Recognizing the capabilities of your people and giving them autonomy will free up your schedule and show them you have confidence in them.

Reflection

- How are you impacting those around you?
- How does your schedule prevent you from building relationships with your team?
- Where are you taking on too much and sending the message that you don't trust your team to get the work done?

Chapter 23

The Promotion

A year after Mike completed the Emerging Leaders Program, Allison asked him to come to her office. She was pleased with his progress, and she had plans for him.

"Mike, how are things going?"

Mike was curious about the question. "I am good. Busy today but lots of great things happening."

Allison grins broadly, looking at the man who she once thought wouldn't be able to do the work to become a fine leader. "You have worked so hard and done so many great things in the last year," she says. "I am thrilled to tell you that you are being promoted to senior director."

WHAT! Mike was speechless. At times, he was still so unsure of himself in the organization. Self-doubt haunted him frequently. "Thank you. I just don't know what to say."

"You have built strong relationships and connections across the whole organization," Allison adds. "You deserve it. Let's go tell the team."

They walked out of Allison's office together. The team is in the cubicles outside of her office. She got everyone's attention and shared the big news. One of the team members cheers and shouts, "This calls for happy hour. Let's go!" The team was so excited for him, and they all headed out to their favorite pub around the corner. During the celebration, many of his peers shared with him fun stories about his journey.

"Remember when Mike first started with the company? He was so out of touch and so uncomfortable in the new environment." Everyone chuckles because they knew it was true. Another person chimes in, "You were so defensive and ready to argue with anyone who gave you feedback." He looks at Mike with a big smile. "You have come a long way!"

Privately, one young woman shares, "I was really disappointed that you got the promotion and not me. I wanted to be in the Emerging Leaders Program so badly! Now that I see how much work you have done and your growth, I am really inspired by you."

Mike was not sure what to say so he just nodded. He was so proud of what he had accomplished and optimistic about his company's future. He had come a long way.

She continues, "I realize now I have work to do. I talked to Allison, and they are letting me go into the next Emerging Leaders class."

Mike was relieved and excited for her. "If you need anything, I am here to help. It is not a complicated class, but it is also not easy to do so much self-reflection!" he offers.

He looked around the room, reflecting on the friends he'd made and the road he had been on that brought him to this place. He could not believe where he was. If you would've told Mike ten years ago that he would be sitting at a happy hour, celebrating the relationships he had made, and the work that he was doing now, he would have called you crazy. *Thank goodness for the messy road. I would not have learned this much if I did not get fired and met Julie for coffee.*

That fateful meeting where he was oddly so open to Julie led him here today. He sent Julie a text message. "I wish you were here today. You will not believe this. I just got a promotion, and it is all thanks to you. Thank you for introducing me to Allison and giving me a chance."

She quickly responds. "Hate to not be there. This is about you and your hard work. Don't dismiss that."

Mike then heads over to sit by Allison. He simply says, "Thank you!"

"For what?" she asks.

"If you were not so open with me sharing your path and the mistakes you made, I might not have been open to doing the work on myself," he adds.

Allison nods. "It is scary. You never know how people will use the stories you tell them. You have to trust that they will take it and learn from it."

Mike agrees. "Now I understand that for me and my leadership, it is about the people. I will build deep relationships."

Like a scene out of a movie and the perfect timing, his new wife, Grace walked in. He was proud of the work that he had done for himself. He was no longer a self-proclaimed forever bachelor. Earlier in his life, he had no clue about the barriers that he was putting up inside and outside of work. Grace hugged her husband. "Congratulations! I knew this day would come."

Allison jumps up to greet Grace.

"I appreciate all the work you've done with Mike," Grace says. "Most people don't know but we went to high school together. He is a different man than the boy in high school."

"That is the best thing. We can all change and grow." Allison winks at Mike and walked away.

Mike chuckles. "Thank goodness I have grown up. You would not give me a chance in high school."

Grace laughs. "Well, that's because you were an asshole."

Mike pretended that what she said hurt his heart, but he knew it was all too true. With a quick kiss, they joined the rest of the group at the bar.

The team went long into the night celebrating. No one wanted to leave. It was such a strong group doing great things.

Be the Catalyst

Each decision we make, the mistakes we make, and the obstacles we overcome makes us stronger and we grow as a leader. Don't limit yourself to the fear of failure or imposter syndrome. Take risks and believe in yourself. We are not the same person we were last year or ten years ago. Resilience and self-awareness allow us to continue to grow. Finally, when we do the work on ourselves, we can have positive impacts on ourselves and our teams.

We must also take time to invest in our people, it helps them grow and impacts the bottom line.

Reflection

- How are you practicing resilience and growth?
- What are some of the risks you've taken and the outcomes?
- What positive impacts do you recognize you've had on the people around you?

Addendum

Self-Determination Theory and The Catalyst Workplace Model

I created the Catalyst Workplace Model during my doctoral research. Through my inquiry on workplace motivation and employee satisfaction, I dove into many motivation theories and chose the self-determination theory.

Edward Deci and Richard Ryan (1985) introduced self-determination theory (SDT) which provides a framework for a person's motivation level. SDT is unique because it explains motivation level as a continuum that a person's motivation moves through based on their experience and the situation they are presented. The theory presents a person's three basic needs of people relatedness, competence, and autonomy. At the very basic level, our employees want a sense of belonging/ community, the tools and training to do the job they were hired to do, and then allowed to do their job.

To promote **relatedness**, leaders should:

1. Focus on company culture to ensure all feel connected and comfortable.
2. Act with authenticity and transparency are key for employees to trust their leadership.

3. Listen and respond when their employees express frustration/concern.

To promote **competence** leaders should:

1. Make sure their team members have the basic tools to complete their job.
2. Provide professional training and development so team members understand their job.
3. Offer personal development opportunities and conversations for growth.

To promote **autonomy**, leaders should:

1. Make sure there is buy-in by all leadership.
2. Ensure policies and procedures for team members to make decisions/resolve issues at the lowest levels.
3. Promote a team environment where all experiences and skills are celebrated.

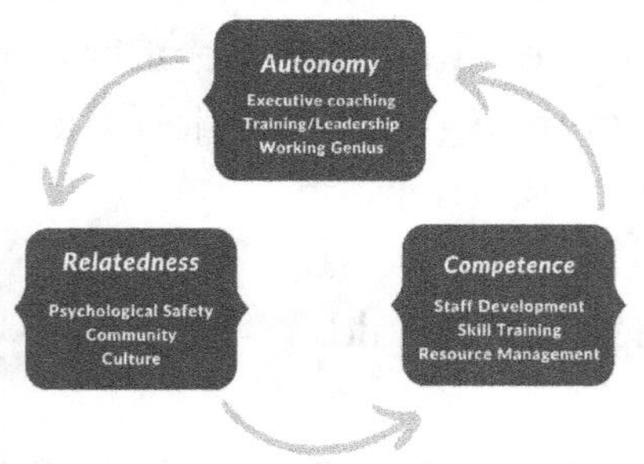

Catalyst Workplace Model

(Ervin, 2018 based on Self Determination Theory; Deci & Ryan, 1985)

Integrated Regulation
Internally motivated
Congruence with the organization
Tasks are personally important
Recognize an external authority

Benefits of Integrated Regulation
Loyalty to the organization/less likely to leave
More engaged in workplace activities
Higher job satisfaction
Happier workplace

What are Career and Power Skills (CAPs)?

At Catalyst Development, when we teach career skills, we base all of our training around intentional skill-building in several important areas.

Soft skills. Power skills. People skills. Career skills. These are all different words to say the same things—and that are critical no matter where we are in our careers. At Catalyst Development, we call them Career and Power Skills. We lean into these skills for all of our clients, whether they are still early in their careers or seasoned executives. While each of these skills is important on its own, we have put them in different buckets and usually teach them in sessions to make them more impactful.

The career and power skill buckets are broken out below:

Lead – How Do You Lead?

- Integrity
- Authenticity
- Humility
- Responsibility
- Dependability
- Commitment
- Self-motivation

Engage – How Do You Communicate?

- Clarity
- Respect
- Verbal/Non-Verbal/Written
- Kindness
- Active listening
- Cooperation

· Coordination

Accept – How Do You Belong?

· Psychological safety
· Unconscious bias
· Trust
· Raising awareness
· Being diversity brave
· Cultural Intelligence
· Cultural Inclusion
· Introvert/Extrovert

Develop – How Do You Work with Others?

· Analysis/logical reasoning
· Lateral thinking
· Initiative/Persistence
· Persuasion
· Negotiation
· Brainstorming/Creativity
· Interpersonal skills
· Silos

Effective – How Do You Get It Done?

· Goal setting
· Prioritizing/planning
· Decision making
· Focus
· Collaboration/Idea exchange
· Organization
· Delegation

Resilient – How Do You Pivot?

- Curiosity
- Agility
- Self-management
- Optimism
- Open-mindedness
- Self-confidence
- Stress management/Coping

We have found that when our clients intentionally work on these vital career skills, they can take their work to the next level. Keep in mind that you can be proficient in some areas and need work in others. To be a strong leader, it is important to be self-aware enough to work on all of them.

Career Skills at All Levels and Stages

Another thing we have learned is that these skills are powerful to us at all stages of life. It's highly beneficial to have a basic understanding of these skills when you're just starting your early career. They will help you make more deliberate moves in your development and build good relationships. Once a person hits what we call the emerging leaders' stage, where they are starting to catch stride in their career, leaning into these career skills can elevate them amongst their peers and prepare them for stretch responsibilities.

The next career stage is mid-career. At Catalyst Development, we like to call these folks strategic leaders. The caution at this stage is that it can also be known as the "frozen middle." It's the place in your career where you're responsible for your team, but you're not the ultimate decision-maker. Depending on the organization, you can get caught in the middle of what your people need and what the executive team will provide.

Mastering your career and power skills can help you manage up and down to build relationships as a whole.

The senior/executive leader level is the one I find doing the least intentional skill-building work. It's understandable. This group has a massive responsibility to run the business, develop its people, and ultimately keep the doors open. As I speak to people at this level, I find two different types. There are those who feel like, "I've got it. I am here at the top, what more can I learn?" Then there is the group that says "I want and need to be a life-long learner, but I don't know how to build my career skills or if I have time to get it done."

No matter where you are in your career and power skills journey, you can always get better. Even if it is thirty minutes a day of intentional reflection, practice, and learning, it's better than staying where you are and not growing!

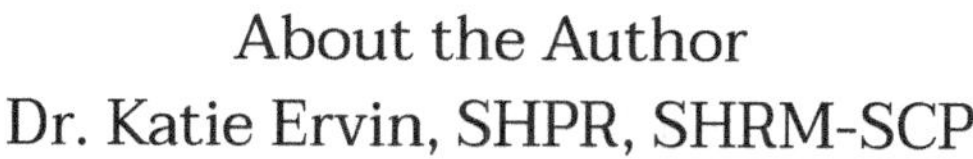

About the Author
Dr. Katie Ervin, SHPR, SHRM-SCP

Dr. Ervin is the founder and CEO of Catalyst Development. Throughout her 22-year career, she has established a reputation as a transformational leader driven by challenge, undeterred by obstacles, and committed to furthering standards of excellence. Dr. Ervin is a vision-driven, goal-focused senior leader with a proven history of innovation and achievement. Her expertise encompasses all aspects of organizational development, from creating efficiencies to controlling costs and maximizing results to harnessing team strengths to improve overall performance. In every organization, her goal is to build consensus to promote transparency and influence positive change. Her work in developing strong leaders and teams focuses on critical career skill building to develop strong cultures and grow organizations.

Dr. Ervin has a unique portfolio of academic, government, corporate, and non-profit experience. With 12 years of both professional and management-level corporate human resources experiences and 11 years in higher education administration, she has focused attention on structuring or restructuring management resources to eliminate waste and repetition, saving organizations thousands of dollars. Through workforce planning, she develops strategies to effectively address recruitment and retention issues and leads efforts in developing and maintaining compensation/performance management systems to ensure companies are competitive locally and nationally. Coupled with her work experience, Dr. Ervin has shared her experience teaching Masters-Level Organizational Development and Human Resources courses for the past

15 years. Her writing is featured as a member of the Forbes Human Resources Council.

Dr. Ervin holds the SHRM Senior Certified Professional and Senior Professional in Human Resources certifications. She is also a certified Working Genius facilitator. She received her Bachelor of Science in Sociology with a minor in Psychology from Pittsburg State University, a Master of Technology in Human Resources Development from Indiana State University, and a Doctorate in Education with an emphasis in Adult Education from Kansas State University. Dr. Ervin's area of research is workplace motivation based on self-determination theory and the impact of an employee's perception of their organization's support. She believes if we meet an employee's basic needs of competence, relatedness, and autonomy, they will be more efficient, happier at work, highly engaged, and more likely to stay with the organization.

Dr. Ervin currently volunteers with the Alzheimer's Association as board chair of the Heart of American Chapter and serves as an active volunteer for her sorority, Alpha Sigma Alpha. She and her husband, Rob, of 22 years, live in Parkville, MO, north of Kansas City, and have two children, Drew and Abby.

More about our work at Catalyst Development

Catalyst Development is rooted in intentional workforce skill-building at all career stages and levels. We can help you build strong teams through our robust learning options, including coaching, speaking, workshops, and full development programs. We heard someone say this and have borrowed it. We are proud to be a company of doing. It is not why you should be a leader but how you be a strong leader!

Our Core Values

Growth: We value lifelong learning, which includes personal and professional development. We believe in being bold in the face of challenges: we are bold enough to admit when we need to change, to have difficult conversations, and to share our stories.

Autonomy: We give ourselves the autonomy to do our jobs in the manner that works for us. Knowing that every team is different, we give our clients autonomy to tell us what they need. We help organizations build trust from within and create autonomy naturally.

Community: We believe in creating an environment where everyone has a seat at the table. We want our friends and clients to feel a sense of belonging. We help our clients create their own communities of belonging, both internally and externally.

Learn how to work with us at www.katieervin.com

9 798218 174071